JOHN WYCLIF AND REFORM

JOHN WYCLIF
AND
REFORM

by

JOHN STACEY

WIPF & STOCK · Eugene, Oregon

Wipf and Stock Publishers
199 W 8th Ave, Suite 3
Eugene, OR 97401

John Wycliff and Reform
By Stacey, John
Copyright©1964 James Clarke & Co
ISBN 13: 978-1-60608-761-9
Publication date 6/1/2009
Previously published by Lutterworth Press, 1964

Contents

Acknowledgments

I AM MOST grateful to the Trustees of the John Rylands Library, Manchester, to the Dr. Williams's Trust, London and to the staff of both these Libraries for their courteous and efficient service. Professor Gordon Rupp of Manchester University, with characteristic generosity, made some invaluable suggestions and the Rev. Rupert Davies, M.A., of Didsbury College, Bristol, kindly gave his judgment on the manuscript. I should like to acknowledge also my debt to Miss Hilary Maines of Timperley and Miss Mary Briant of Pitshanger for long hours of hard work at the typewriter and to Miss Audrey Byers who read the proofs.

J. S.

Greenford,
Middlesex.
February, 1964.

CHAPTER ONE

John Wyclif

THE SOURCES TO which one would naturally turn to assess the character of John Wyclif are his written works and the testimony of his biographers. There are difficulties with both. His published writings, consisting of some forty works in ecclesiastical Latin and a lesser number in English, are impersonal throughout and offer little indication of the kind of man he was. He allows his affection for Oxford to be known. "The house of God and the gate of heaven" he calls it and he eulogizes the meadows and streams and balmy air which he found there[1], but such disclosures are most infrequent and one peruses in vain the pages of scholastic and theological argument in search of information about the man, John Wyclif. More human documents such as letters to personal friends have either perished or were never written. After a lifetime devoted to the study of his works Professor Shirley describes him as an author "without personality or expression" and K. B. McFarlane, his brilliant modern critic, says that he lives "as a force more than as a man".[2]

For the biographer Wyclif is a controversial figure because he stands at the parting of the ways. His denunciation of the medieval Church, made with such vigour and pungency, and his profession of some of the ecclesiastical and theological tenets associated with the Protestant Reformation have meant that biographers and historians have from the start judged him from the preconceptions of their own theology. High and low churchmen both confess to this. Dom David Knowles makes the comment that "no historian has yet been able to approach him with perfect sobriety of judgment"[3] and H. B. Workman, his Methodist biographer, complains that "his name has been the sport of excited partisans".[4] Such treatment does not facilitate an impartial assessment of the man's character. Just how difficult that is to achieve is shown by Peter Heylin who, in his Preface to *Examen Historicum*, laments that "whole Histories are composed with so much partiality . . . that they stand in need of a Commentator to expound the Truth and lay it clear and open to the view of the Reader", and yet finds it quite impossible to avoid an anti-Wyclif bias.

The bare facts of Wyclif's life need at this point to be stated. He was born in the North Riding of Yorkshire about 1330 and began his education at Oxford while still quite young. His name has been associated with three colleges, Queen's, Merton and Balliol. A John Wyclif hired lodgings at Queen's for some five years between 1363 and 1381 and as such an arrangement would have suited the studies and parish duties of the scholar from Yorkshire, this would appear to be a reference to him, though there is mention of an "almonry boy" of the same name at Queen's in 1371. Merton College has a record of "John Wyclif" as a steward and junior fellow in 1356, but it has been argued that Merton was a southern college, unlikely to receive a northerner, and there is the additional difficulty of explaining why Wyclif, if it was he, left the comparative luxury of Merton for a less lucrative position at Balliol. These arguments require the existence of another John Wyclif to account for the Merton record and a claimant has been put forward in the person of John Whitclif, Vicar of Mayfield, who was appointed to that position by the Archbishop of Canterbury, himself a Merton man. The evidence is not conclusive either way.

Between 1356 and 1360 John Wyclif was elected the third Master of Balliol and it is presumed that this implies previous residence as a scholar, but he resigned his Mastership in 1361 when he was instituted at Holbeach in Lincolnshire to the college living of Fillingham. There has been considerable debate as to whether or not Wyclif was Warden of Canterbury

Hall, a house for secular and regular clergy at Oxford founded by Archbishop Islip in 1361. Two contemporary writers, a chronicler at St. Albans and the Franciscan, William Woodford, say that he was. On the other hand Wyclif writes of Canterbury Hall in *De Ecclesia*[5] with feeling, but without any sense of personal attachment (though this is usual), and the enigmatic Whitclif of Mayfield must again be considered because of his connections with Islip. However, as several scholars have pointed out,[6] the evidence in the Mayfield man's favour is circumstantial only and a strong case exists for the older view. There was considerable trouble at Canterbury Hall between the seculars and the regulars, but it was finally settled by a papal judgment which went against Wyclif.

By 1360 Wyclif had become a regent master in arts at Balliol. His departure for Fillingham was followed in 1362 by a petition from the University to the Pope to "provide" for him, along with other masters, and he was given a prebend at Aust in the collegiate church of Westbury-on-Trym, near Bristol. In 1363 and 1368 he was granted licences from the Bishop of Lincoln to absent himself from Fillingham to study at Oxford, though in 1368 he exchanged Fillingham for Ludgershall, a parish nearer the University. His studies at this time were theological and he took his B.D. about 1369 and his D.D. in 1372, residing for the purpose at Queen's. In 1373 Gregory XI renewed the grant from a "provision" of a canonry in Lincoln reserved for Wyclif a year or two earlier, though whether he actually received the £45 per annum it was worth is doubtful.[7] On April 7, 1374, Edward III presented him to the rectory of Lutterworth in place of Ludgershall.

The same year Wyclif received a commission in the service of the Crown and was appointed to the deputation to discuss with the papal representatives at Bruges the outstanding differences between England and Rome, but the conference achieved little and Wyclif returned to Oxford to study and to write his political treatises on Divine and Civil Dominion. His next excursion into politics was as the ally of John of

Gaunt, who from motives less scrupulous than those of Wyclif was opposed to the wealth and power of the clergy. Wyclif preached in London in support of moderate disendowment and the people heard him gladly, but this action and his general approval of Gaunt's anti-clerical policy exposed him to the strong opposition of Courtenay, Bishop of London, and the more timid Sudbury, Archbishop of Canterbury. Wyclif appeared before them both at St. Paul's in February, 1377, but the proceedings broke up in disorder and Wyclif retired unmolested and uncondemned.

He was not uncondemned for long. Three months after the scuffle in St. Paul's the Pope, probably informed by Benedictine monks, issued five Bulls against Wyclif in the course of which eighteen errors were denounced, mostly concerning Divine and Civil Dominion. Sudbury, Courtenay, the University of Oxford and Edward III were urged to expedite the arrest of the "master of errors", but the papal proclamations did not command the unquestioning obedience of their recipients. Edward III died and the others, Courtenay excepted, found discretion to be the better part of valour, for Wyclif was at the height of his popularity and influence. (His opinion was sought by the King's Council as to whether or not it was lawful to keep the treasure of the kingdom from Rome.) Oxford refused to condemn her outstanding scholar, though Wyclif consented to a "house-arrest" in Black Hall to save the University from punitive action by the Pope. He refused to appear at St. Paul's within thirty days, as Sudbury and Courtenay wished, but consented to face the bishops at Lambeth later in 1378. Here he had the support of a message from the Queen Mother, the sympathy of the government and the intervention on his behalf of the citizens of London. The trial produced only an innocuous warning.

Wyclif's last political appearance was in the autumn of 1378. Robert Haulay, an English knight, had been killed at Westminster Abbey after a complicated dispute over a Spanish hostage. The crucial question was the Right of Sanctuary. Wyclif appeared before Parliament at Gloucester to plead for the Crown against the injustices of the Sanctuary privilege, but no decision was reached.

1378 was the year of the Great Schism and a decisive one for Wyclif. The spectacle of two Vicars of Christ, one excommunicating the other, appalled him, and he became in ever-increasing measure a rebel, at a time when the divided Church could not risk taking action against him. Then his mind began to turn to the central theological doctrines of the Church, and he published opinions, later deemed heretical, concerning the Eucharist, bringing down upon himself the wrath of the friars. He continued to denounce the evils of the Church and did not shrink from the theological consequences of his diatribes. He became Wyclif the heretic.

The tension produced by this course of action was soon felt at Oxford. In 1380 the Chancellor summoned a small council to examine Wyclif's eucharistic teaching and by seven votes it was condemned, though discussion and debate continued throughout the University. From August 1380 until the summer of the following year Wyclif was in his rooms at Queen's, busy doubtless with his writing, his plans for a translation of the Bible and for the foundation of an order of Poor Preachers who could take Bible truth to the people. In 1381 he retired to his parish at Lutterworth.

That year the discontent of the labouring classes burst its banks in the Peasants' Revolt, but Wyclif's teachings, as yet known almost exclusively to the learned, were not instrumental in any appreciable way in causing it. The statement by Varillas that John Ball "went to seek out Wickliffe who received him with open arms"[8] is uncorroborated and Froissart, the contemporary historian of the Revolt, has nothing to say about Wyclif. The most that can be alleged is that his natural sympathies lay with the oppressed. Conversely, the effect of the Revolt on him was considerable. There was a *rapprochement* between the Church and the State in the face of the common danger, and this meant the end of Wyclif's alliance with John of Gaunt and so of what political influence he had had. Worse still, Sudbury was murdered in the Revolt and the vigorous Courtenay was made Archbishop, and he soon moved against Wyclif. On May 17, 1382, a special committee was summoned to Blackfriars and examined twenty-four Conclusions from Wyclif's works, ten of which it found heretical and fourteen erroneous. The Council finished in the apocalyptic atmosphere of an earthquake. Courtenay followed this up with a successful appeal to the temporal power to give the bishops all possible assistance in restraining the growing influence of Lollardry, then turned to Oxford, overcame the resistance of Rigg the Chancellor, secured the capitulation of most of Wyclif's followers in the University and had all his writings banned.

Wyclif spent the last two and a half years of his life in the parish at Lutterworth unmolested in person (possibly due to the influence of John of Gaunt who might have spoken up for his former ally), and writing books and pamphlets with the fury of a man whose pen has little time to glean his teeming brain. In 1382 he suffered his first stroke and was left partly paralysed, and for this reason was unable to answer a citation to Rome. On Holy Innocents' Day, 1384, he was smitten with another severe stroke as he was hearing Mass at Lutterworth and he died three days later on December 31. He was buried in consecrated ground as he had never been excommunicated, but in 1482 Richard Fleming, Bishop of Lincoln, obeyed the order of the Council of Constance, dug up the bones of John Wyclif, burnt them, and threw them into the River Swift.

It is one thing to record the facts of Wyclif's life but quite another to evaluate those facts and so form a sound judgment about him. What sort of a man was he? His admirers and his critics reach a wide variety of conclusions. There are those who see him as the first Protestant hero, fighting almost alone the hosts of medieval wickedness, and for them he is the Morning Star heralding a brighter and a better day; the "worthy precursor of the German Reformation", as Reinhold Pauli puts it.[9] "This aforesaid Wickliffe, by God's providence, sprang and rose up, through whom the Lord would first waken and raise up again the world",[10] is how Foxe reads the fourteenth century. "In the spirit of this wonderful man," writes Buddensieg, "Protestantism arose",[11] and F. C. Massingberd, who holds that "that old and glorious title of *Ecclesia Anglicana* is no modern invention", calls him "Father of the Reformation".[12] He has, in their eyes, all the virtues of the true Reformer. "A fierce enquirer after truth", wrote William Gilpin in 1765, "and a steady maintainer of it when discovered".[13] All his admirers extol his virtuous life. They never weary of quoting Archbishop Arundel's admission to the Lollard, William Thorpe: "Wyclif your author was a great clerk and many men held him a perfect liver." Thorpe, in his examination as recorded by Bale, pays his own tribute, *"Magister Joannes Wiclevus habebatur a multis omnium aetate sua viventium sanctissimus"* and Foxe's version of this is "Maister John Wickliffe was holden of full mainie men the greatest clerke that they then knew living, and therewith he was named a passing rulie man and an innocent in his living."[14] The truth of this all friendly commentators have stoutly maintained. "His excellent piety", wrote Wharton, "even the worst and most spiteful of his adversaries never dared to call in question."[15] Robert Vaughan writes a typical sentence: "The impression indeed, which must be made by a candid and adequate attention to the history and writings of Wycliffe, is not only that his piety is that of the scriptures, but that it resulted from a strength of faith, and was distinguished by an unearthliness of feeling, which are of no frequent occurrence in the annals of the Church."[16]

This admiration can best be seen in the constant tributes to Wyclif's singlemindedness. His champions lean over backwards to show that his "provisions" and preferments were received and held from the highest motives. Wyclif's move from Fillingham to Ludgershall, which McFarlane suggests was, like that of any "chop-church", to raise money,[17] is described by Workman as "a desire on Wyclif's part to keep more oversight over his flock than was possible at Fillingham."[18] Then there was the matter of the prebend at Aust. Wyclif was undoubtedly an absentee who used the resources of the prebend to maintain himself at Oxford and failed to appoint a vicar in his place, and this has led at least one modern critic to say, "The estimate of Wyclif's character in the past has been too high".[19] Yet R. L. Poole asserts (wrongly) that Wyclif soon resigned the prebend and gives as the reason, "possibly from some scruple about the tenure of benefices in plurality".[20] Wyclif's move from Oxford to Lutterworth, made at a time when the University was rapidly becoming too hot for him, is attributed by W. H. Freemantle, somewhat benignly, to "the effort to raise the common life by pastoral intercourse".[21] One more example will suffice. When Wyclif began to deny the doctrine of Transubstantiation, his old ally, John of Gaunt, hurried to Oxford to silence him. But Wyclif would not be silenced. On the contrary, his attack grew fiercer. His critics attribute this to intransigent obstinacy and a wilful political blindness which prevented his seeing that no reform was possible without the active co-operation of John of Gaunt and his kind. Not so his admirers. G. M. Trevelyan, for instance, argues that this was an example of great sacrifice for the sake of principle.[22] Wyclif threw away the protection which the government and nobility could have given him and was driven from his beloved Oxford rather than deny, even by silence, the truth which he felt it his mission to proclaim. "A man of war from his youth up, the truth was always more to him than peace".[23] This singlemindedness is acclaimed from all sides. As H. B. Workman says, "Wyclif himself was real: his bitterest foes could not label him otherwise".[24]

To this must be added all the other compliments paid him by friendly biographers, of which the following are typical. Lewis Sergeant compares him with John Knox: "And the same epitaph might be written over the grave of each— 'Here lies one who never feared the face of man'."[25] Dr. Lechler quotes Chaucer's description of the humble, conscientious country priest from the Prologue to the *Canterbury Tales* and continues: "There are several features of this portrait which agree with the character of Wycliffe and not a single trait can be detected in it which does not suit him. The humility, the contentment, and the unselfishness; the moral spotlessness, the compassionate love, the conscientious and diligent faithfulness in his office, and the Biblical character of his preaching—these lineaments were all his".[26] "One of the greatest men our country has produced", writes Dean Hook.[27] John Wyclif has not gone unappreciated.

On the other hand he has not lacked his enemies and critics. In his own day these were drawn from the ranks of the monks and friars who were concerned both to retaliate against his strong denunciations of them ("His evil and baleful teaching against the religious monks and mendicants"[28] as William Woodford called it), and to stand as the champions of catholic orthodoxy. One of his first opponents was Frater Johannes Kynyngham, a Carmelite who argued with him for some years on a variety of subjects ranging from the truth of Scripture to the doctrine that whatever has been, or will be, is. The Black Monks in the provincial Chapter of Durham attempted to set up John de Acley as an official apologist against Wyclif, a course which was only stopped by government action. The kind of opinion that the religious entertained of Wyclif can be seen in this extract from *Chronicon Angliae*,[29] written by a monk of St. Albans:

> . . . a certain false devine, or as I may better name hym, a fyghter agaynste God, whoe, many years before, in all hys acts in the scholes had barked agaynste the churche . . . and many new opynions he invented without any grounds but suche which vaynly occupied the eares of the herers. Thys felow was called John, but unworthely, for that he had caste away the grace that God had givean hym. . . . He was not only eloquent but also a most perfect hypocryte and dyssembler, directynge all hys doyings to one ende, thát ys to witt to spreade hys worde, hys fame and opynion amongst men.

There was no love lost on Wyclif the heretic, and Adam of Usk spoke of him as Mahomet. Henry Knighton, a monk of Leicester, the author of a contemporary Chronicle, records a recantation by Wyclif; but this is wishful thinking, unsubstantiated by any accurate record of events. Another early opponent was Thomas Netter of Walden, a Carmelite whose work, collected in *Fasciculi Zizaniorum*, has for long been one of the principal sources of information about Wyclif. He was responsible for propagating the innuendo that Wyclif's outburst of heresy was due to his chagrin at not obtaining the bishopric of Worcester, and he began to describe what he believed to be the errors of Wyclif under the text St. Matthew 13: 28: *"Inimicus homo hoc fecit"*.[30] The *Historia Anglicana* of Thomas Walsingham, another monk connected with St. Albans, is strongly prejudiced against Wyclif, refers to his "erroneous and heretical conclusions, lying and absurd, against the universal laws of the Church",[31] and calls him "an old hypocrite, an angel of Satan". Abuse poured forth from the monastery at St. Albans and such terms as "devil's instrument", "church's enemy", "people's confusion", "heretics' idol", "flatteries' sink", were some of the more forthright. The monastic historians were not sympathetic.

Such radical criticism grew less as Europe approached the Reformation. Most post-Reformation biographies and comments are eulogies of the Morning Star. There are exceptions, like the violent language of Matthias Earbery (1690–1740), a non-juror who included Wyclif amongst his considerable array of enemies. He translated the *Histoire du Wiclefianisme* of Varillas and after describing Wyclif in his Preface as "a wicked Man whose notions were abominable", he translated with evident relish the critical words of Varillas. The charges are the usual ones. Because he was denied a bishop's throne Wyclif "fought for means to avenge himself on the pope . . . fill'd his Mind with the Sentiments of the later Hereticks . . . and delivered these new Doctrines with an artful Vehemence"[32] The book is scurrilous and inaccurate. It called forth in 1688 *Reflections upon Mr. Varillas, His History of Heresy* (Burnet, Hannes and King), in which Varillas was accused of using his pen with "a partial Extravagance and with so little regard to Modesty and Truth". A detailed attempt is made to rehabilitate Wyclif, in the course of which the accusation about preferment is stoutly denied. A further reply along the same lines followed from the pen of John Lewis in 1719. Anthony Wood, another seventeenth-century critic, had his own version of the "sour grapes" theory. Wyclif, he said, was ejected from Canterbury Hall and, "upon the loss thereof, he was soe much stirred up to revenge that afterwards he raised commotion in the church and was the author of many haeretical tenets".[33] This hostile approach was shared by Dr. Fell, Wood's contemporary, who remarked, "John Wycleve was a grand dissembler, a man of little conscience, and what he did as to religion was more out of vainglory and to obtain unto him a name, than out of honesty".[34]

In the modern era we meet again the devastating criticism which tears down the Protestant idol. Dr. John Lingard, a Roman Catholic who wrote a History of England in 1849, not unnaturally disliked Wyclif. "In common with other religious innovators", he writes, "he claimed the two-fold privilege of changing his opinions at will and of being infallible in every change".[35] Dr. F. J. C. Hearnshaw damns Wyclif by maintaining that he was not a religious man at all. He had "no religious experience, no sense of sin, no consciousness of conversion, no assurance of salvation, no heart of love, no evident communion with God",[36] but was rather "a thinker whose interest in his theme was purely moral and intellectual".

K. B. McFarlane is *par excellence* the modern critic of this kind, and his small but scintillating book does its best to rid the uncritical admirer of his delusions. The comment on Wyclif's printed works reveals McFarlane's unsentimental approach: "One gathers little more from them than that their author was learned, subtle, ingenious, opinionated, tirelessly argumentative and rather humourless"[37] . . . "that they are also abusive and cantankerous is hardly surprising since they are the works of a bitter old man in a hurry. Most of Wycliffe's later writings are offensive, his attempts, not always overscrupulous attempts, to destroy his opponents' case and to maintain his own".[38] McFarlane argues that it is possible to believe in Wyclif's absolute sincerity as a reformer, "while at the same time suspecting that a plum or two, even as late as the early 1370s, might have shut his mouth for ever".[39] One doubts whether McFarlane himself concedes the sincerity of Wyclif, particularly when he asserts that the psychological explanation of his rebellion was the "bad grace" and the "sense of persecution" which he harboured as a result of his failure to climb the ecclesiastical ladder. He reports too Hallam's tale, propagated by Netter, about Wyclif's heresies having their origin in his disappointment over the bishopric of Worcester (Hastings Rashdall calls the tale "a malicious suggestion"), and says it is "at least credible". Moreover it is difficult to reconcile a recognition of Wyclif's sincerity with the "preferable guess" that "his head, never strong . . . was turned by his success as a disputant and preacher and by the flattering attentions of the great"[40] or with the jibe, "it needed the threat of persecution to turn the politician into a heretic; the truth alone had had no such compulsive force".[41] Despite a specific claim to acknowledge singlemindedness,[42] there is little recognition of it in the suggestion that Wyclif attacked the doctrine of Transubstantiation, not when he became convinced of its falsity, but when it suited his convenience. Although many of Wyclif's attainments are conceded, his ability in the schools and his personal simplicity for example, the Wyclif of these pages is a very different man from the Protestant hero of earlier biographers.

The question "Which is the real John Wyclif?" is perhaps unanswerable after six hundred years. The most one can do is to try to correct excesses of one kind or another by as cautious and objective an approach as possible.

We must be prepared to concede the sincerity of John Wyclif. He was on occasions mistaken and proud, but he was not insincere. The attack on the Church, to which we shall turn more fully later, gives one the overall impression that its author was moved much more by moral earnestness and a genuine desire for reform than by the angry spleen of a disappointed ecclesiastic, though this is not to deny the

occasional presence of the latter. The relevant paragraph of
Acts and Monuments is not far from the truth:

> This Wickliff after he had now a long time professed divinity
> in the University of Oxford, and perceiving the true doctrine
> of Christ's gospel to be adulterated and defiled with so many
> filthy inventions of bishops, sects of monks, and dark errors:
> and that he, after long debating and deliberating with himself
> (with many secret sighs, and bewailing in his mind the general
> ignorance of the whole world), could no longer suffer or abide
> the same, at the last determined with himself to remedy such
> things as he saw to be wide and out of the way.[43]

In this matter the truth as he saw it had for Wyclif compulsive force. Certainly when his attack turned friends into
enemies, as in the case of the friars and his (to them) heretical
doctrine of the Eucharist, he made no attempt whatever to
keep his allies by accommodating his views to theirs, and,
as we have noticed, he paid little attention to John of Gaunt
and so lost much of his support. This is better explained by
the sincerity of his convictions than by the assumption that
he was so perverse that he did not care whether he had allies
or not. His life as we know it has no instance of his drawing
back from any action for fear of the consequences, and a critic
like Hearnshaw concedes this willingly and admits that his
solitary stand against all comers "argues a courage little less
than sublime".[44] It is hard to see how this can be reconciled
with insincerity. Perhaps he was headstrong, impulsive
and not wise enough always to count the cost, but of his
sincerity there can be no reasonable doubt. This is not to say
that he was invariably consistent. For one thing, his work,
both destructive and constructive, was not a carefully planned
and completely integrated whole, for he was a "red-hot"
reformer who spoke and wrote as the spirit seized him and as
evil and error were borne in upon him, and this was the
reason he attacked the doctrine of Transubstantiation just
when he did. This explains too the considerable difference
between his earlier and later writings.

Then there is the matter of inconsistency in his life. He was
severe in his denunciation of absenteeism amongst the

clergy and he disapproved of those who left their flocks, "by serving in official secular negotiations, taking their ease in the schools, making illicit journeys or visiting the Roman pontiff".[45] Yet Wyclif was absent from Westbury without appointing a vicar in his place and his visit to Bruges in 1374 was nothing else but "official secular negotiations". However, such instances, though common practice at the time, are most infrequent in his life and all the industrious attempts of critics both ancient and modern to find more have been unsuccessful. We have then no adequate reasons for rejecting the judgment of his admirers that Wyclif was a sincere man who believed passionately in all he said and did.

Side by side with sincerity in John Wyclif's character there was a certain ingenuousness and lack of worldly wisdom. His life is full of examples of an almost childish impracticability. There was his excursion into politics where, for a time, he became a tool in the hands of John of Gaunt (not "the expert ally" as H. A. L. Fisher describes him).[46] When in 1376 Lancaster was packing Parliament and arranging for the trial of the great William of Wykeham for negligence as a minister, Wyclif was preaching hard in the pulpits of London. Whether he was denouncing the worldliness of the clergy, as his friends contend, or slandering William of Wykeham, as his enemies suggest, or both, he was doing what John of Gaunt wanted him to do. This was due not to cowardice but to ignorance of politicians and their ways. Wyclif was prepared to stand alone against the world when he knew what he was doing, but in this case he did not. As Heseltine says, "He did not so much choose his friends as his friends chose him."[47] The admiring Workman compares him to the idealistic Oxford don who (in Workman's day!) represented his University in the House of Commons, and the comparison can be allowed. In the stormy seas of fourteenth-century politics Wyclif was soon out of his depth, for he lacked the subtle scheming and far-sighted worldly wisdom so necessary for the politician and no historian regrets that he soon turned from his politics to his books.

The same characteristic can be seen in his apparent

disregard of the practical consequences of events, as, for example, the loss of Oxford. The year 1382 saw a determined attempt by Archbishop Courtenay to suppress Wycliffism at Oxford. Mandates, discourses, sermons, disputations and menacing letters were the weapons, and the fight was hard. The victory went to Courtenay and it was of some significance, for Lollardry lost its hold on the most influential place in Britain and its original scholarly character could not then last for long. During this vital year Wyclif was at Lutterworth, preaching to his rural congregation and writing his treatises and pamphlets, apparently unconcerned about the loss of Oxford and what it meant for the cause of reform. There may be other reasons, but the most likely is that he was not far-seeing enough in matters of policy to assess the importance of what was happening.

We shall find this same ingenuousness when we come to examine his politico-ecclesiastical theories. As theories they are not without their importance, but his attempts to relate them to fourteenth-century society were deficient in worldly wisdom and they confirm the impression that he was a sincere but not a practical man.

Another feature of Wyclif's character was a tempestuous nature combined with a sustained capacity for invective. Few writers have damned their opponents' opinions, and sometimes, it would appear, the opponents themselves, more thoroughly. The Pope, the cardinals, the "Caesarean" clergy (clergy in secular and usually well-paid employment), the monks and the friars all received what Knowles calls "this sour legacy of hatred".[48] As William Gilpin, who admired Wyclif greatly, says of his attacks on the court of Rome: "It was his favourite topic and seldom failed, however coolly he might begin, to give him warmth and spirit as he proceeded".[49] This is to put it mildly, for the language used was strong. The Pope, particularly after the Great Schism of 1378, was castigated with phrases like "Cristis enemye . . . poison under colour of Holynesse".[50] "So the wicked pope is anti-Christian and a devil, for he is both falsehood itself and the father of lies".[51] One might continue

JOHN WYCLIF AND REFORM

through the entire hierarchy. Of the cardinals it can be said: "More foul pride and coveitise is in no Lord of the world";[52] the "Caesarean" clergy "that press to be Chancellor and Treasurer and Governors of all worldly offices in the kingdom" are "traitors of God and his people";[53] the monks "love . . . their own belly";[54] the friars are "Ypocritis" full of "Stynkinge covetise", "Hatid and cursid of God" who propagate "foule heresie" and suffer people "in hor synnes, for wynninge of stinkynge muck and lustis of hor owne bely, that is foule wormes meete and a sack of dritt".[55] One could quote page after page of blistering invective in which the clergy of the medieval Church came under the lash of Wyclif's tongue, and then conclude with the Carmelite, John Cunningham, "It is a wonder to me that such a virtuous man uses such language".[56]

Wyclif was no less severe on the customs of which he disapproved. Relic worship, "an irregular and greedy cult", the extortion of exorbitant marriage fees, "this olde roton synne", simony of all kinds, "cursed heresie for it presumeth to selle the Holy Gost", the dispensing of the treasure of the accumulated merits of the saints, "this foolish fantasy . . . dreamed without ground", are typical examples which could be repeated *ad nauseam*. Wyclif spoke his mind with the strongest language at his command.

Varied judgments have been made on these lengthy diatribes. Rudolph Buddensieg, who edited the *Polemical Works*, has made perhaps the most charitable. "But with all the sharpness of the contest, with all the moral earnestness of the patriot and the Christian, the language remains full of a noble pathos, and never descends to the reckless and fanatical declamation which . . . we are led [by his critics] to expect".[57] But there is little of "noble pathos" when Wyclif really turns on his enemies. He detests them for their obvious misdeeds, but he detests them just the same. A quite different assessment is made by McFarlane. He dismisses these indignant outbursts as "the veriest commonplaces of fourteenth-century controversy",[58] and will not allow them as evidence for reforming zeal, and that there is truth in this even Workman admits. "The violence of his language which has shocked many is chiefly borrowed from . . . current polemics".[59] If we do not partially share this view we are committing Wyclif, amongst other things, to a strong personal hatred for Gregory XI, but to regard all his outpourings as the mere stock-in-trade of "a controversialist in hardship" does not do justice to the earnestness of his protest.

Three further observations need to be made. The first is that Wyclif never relied on abuse alone. He argued his case every time. His jibe that "if a friar blesses a cask in the cellar he turns it into accidents without substance" must be taken with his monumental philosophical arguments on the subject of Transubstantiation. The second is the point made by James in 1608 in his "Apologie for John Wycliffe, shewing his conformitie with the now Church of England", that Wyclif "notes abuses in general; he never names any one of his adversaries, monk or friar". Though this charity is not always extended to the Papacy, it is true that there is a commendable absence of personal animosity in the works of Wyclif. The third is that Wyclif had the grace to confess his weakness. "I too readily impart a sinister, vindicative zeal into my legitimate line of argument, if I may be said to have any . . . As for the imputation of hypocrisy, hatred and rancour under a pretence of holiness, I fear, and I admit it with sorrow, this has happened to me too frequently".[60] The substance of this is repeated in *De Civili Dominio* and there he adds, "I confess my sin sorrowing, but I ask my God for grace".[61] Dean Hook's assertion that he "explained away" his most intemperate statements is not the happiest way of commenting upon this, and G. G. Coulton is more fair. "His weakest point, perhaps, was that asperity which he himself confessed publicly with regret".[62]

There is a puritanical streak in the character of John Wyclif. He disliked any ritual which, by its complications, took the mind away from the central truth behind it. "God forbid that any Christian man understand that this censing and crying that men use now be the best service of a priest and most profitable to a man's soul". "It seems that we seek our own liking and pride in this song more than the devotion and understanding of that which we sing, and this is great sin".[63] Too much decoration and magnificence of architecture, he thought, distracted the worshipper. B. L. Manning makes the interesting point that such a puritanical spirit was "a marked characteristic of fourteenth-century religion",[64] and he collects evidence to prove his case, like the quaint rhyme,

> Daunces, Karols, somour games,
> Of many swych come many shames
> Whan thou stodyst to make thyse
> Thou art slogh yn Goddys seruyse.

However, even if we grant Manning his point, Wyclif's puritanical attitude cannot be adequately explained by assuming that he was merely conforming to the outlook of his time because there was a severity in his character which would have made him a puritan in any age.

Against these tendencies to harshness and rigour must be set his interest in and concern for the poor. Here we notice a warm humanity which those who would dismiss him as a bad-tempered intellectual must take into account. He undoubtedly had the welfare of the poor peasants at heart. His social teaching was not a significant cause of the Peasants' Revolt in 1381 and he had no hand in the course of events, but there is no doubt where his sympathies were. In *De Blasphemia* he argued that though the peasants acted cruelly (which could hardly be denied), the people really to blame were the clergy, and the punishment inflicted upon them, though too severe, was not undeserved.[65] Scholars have not been slow to contrast the respective attitudes of Wyclif and Luther to peasants in revolt, to Wyclif's undoubted advantage. Wyclif resented Christian charity being lavished upon the mendicant orders when the proper recipients should be the deserving poor. "But Christ has specified in His law who should have such alms . . . poor men and blind, poor men and lame, poor men and feeble, that

JOHN WYCLIF

need such help".[66] Whether or not the famous translation of the Bible associated with his name was made principally to meet the needs of the uneducated is a matter for consideration later, but such a motive cannot have been entirely absent, as it could not have been from his conception of the order of Poor Priests. This concern for the poor has made some of his admirers link his name with that of St. Francis, but they recognize that the similarity between the two men was only at this point. With Wyclif it never really left the security of the ivory tower for the dust of the arena.

From evidence of this kind no full and comprehensive account of the character of the blunt Yorkshireman can be given and, as has been pointed out, the causes of this are the impersonal nature of his writings and the controversial position he has occupied in both history and theology. We cannot estimate his character from his face because no surviving portrait is authentic. We can only accept certain characteristics as factual and proceed to examine the contribution to Reform that was made by such a man.

REFERENCES

1. De fratribus ad scholares. Opera Minora, p. 18.
2. JOHN WYCLIFFE AND THE BEGINNINGS OF ENGLISH NON-CONFORMITY, K. B. McFarlane, p. 188.
3. THE RELIGIOUS ORDERS IN ENGLAND, vol. II: "The End of the Middle Ages", David Knowles, p. 98.
4. JOHN WYCLIF, A STUDY OF THE ENGLISH MEDIEVAL CHURCH, vol. II, H. B. Workman, p. 321.
5. De Ecclesia, p. 371. He refers to it as unum collegium in Oxonia.
6. H. S. Cronin, JOHN WYCLIFFE, THE REFORMER, AND CANTERBURY HALL, OXFORD. Trans. R.H.S., vol. VIII, 3rd series, p. 71; Bernard Manning, CAMBRIDGE MEDIEVAL HISTORY, vol. VII, p. 487.

7. See H. S. Cronin, WYCLIFFE'S CANONRY AT LINCOLN. E.H.S., vol. 35 (1920), p. 564 ff.

8. *Histoire du Wiclefianisme*, Varillas. Trans. under title: THE PRETENDED REFORMERS OR THE HISTORY OF THE HERESIE OF JOHN WICKLIFFE, JOHN HUSS AND JEROM OF PRAGUE, M. Earbery, p. 25.

9. PICTURES OF OLD ENGLAND, R. Pauli, p. 292.

10. ACTS AND MONUMENTS OF JOHN FOXE, vol. II, p. 796.

11. JOHN WICLIF, PATRIOT AND REFORMER, R. Buddensieg, p. 13.

12. THE ENGLISH REFORMATION, F. C. Massingberd, p. vii.

13. THE LIVES OF JOHN WYCLIF AND OF THE MOST EMINENT OF HIS DISCIPLES, W. Gilpin, p. 5.

14. *Fasciculi Zizaniorum*, Ed. W. W. Shirley, p. xlv.

15. Appendix to Cave's *Historia Literaria: Saeculum Wicklevianum*, p. 62.

16. THE LIFE AND OPINIONS OF JOHN DE WYCLIFFE, D.D., vol. II, Robert Vaughan, p. 373.

17. McFarlane, p. 29.

18. Workman, vol. I, p. 195.

19. Cronin, Trans. R.H.S., vol. VIII, 3rd series, p. 57.

20. WYCLIFFE AND MOVEMENTS FOR REFORM, R. L. Poole, p. 76.

21. PROPHETS OF THE CHRISTIAN FAITH, W. H. Freemantle, p. 99.

22. ENGLAND IN THE AGE OF WYCLIFFE, G. M. Trevelyan, p. 174.

23. Ibid., p. 175.

24. THE DAWN OF THE REFORMATION, vol. I: "The Age of Wyclif", H. B. Workman, p. 149.

25. JOHN WYCLIF, LAST OF THE SCHOOLMEN AND FIRST OF THE ENGLISH REFORMERS, Lewis Sergeant, p. 4.

26. JOHN WYCLIFFE AND HIS ENGLISH PRECURSORS, G. V. Lechler, p. 207.

27. LIVES OF THE ARCHBISHOPS, vol. III, W. F. Hook, p. 76.

28. *Fasciculi Zizaniorum*, p. 518.

29. Published in *Archaelogia*, vol. XXII.

30. *Fasciculi Zizaniorum*, p. 1.

31. *Historia Anglicana*, p. 188.
32. THE PRETENDED REFORMERS, pp. 5-7.
33. SURVEY OF THE ANTIQUITIES OF THE CITY OF OXFORD, vol. II, Anthony Wood, p. 284.
34. Wood's LIFE, p. 81.
35. HISTORY OF ENGLAND, vol. III, John Lingard, p. 153.
36. THE SOCIAL AND POLITICAL IDEAS OF SOME GREAT MEDIEVAL THINKERS, F. J. C. Hearnshaw, p. 222.
37. McFarlane, p. 10.
38. Ibid., p. 86.
39. Ibid., p. 27.
40. Ibid., p. 85.
41. Ibid., p. 84.
42. Ibid., p. 36.
43. ACTS AND MONUMENTS OF JOHN FOXE, vol. II, p. 796.
44. THE SOCIAL AND POLITICAL IDEAS OF SOME GREAT MEDIEVAL THINKERS, p. 223.
45. *De Blasphemia*, p. 178.
46. HISTORY OF EUROPE, vol. I, H. A. L. Fisher, p. 350.
47. GREAT YORKSHIREMEN, G. C. Heseltine, p. 220.
48. THE RELIGIOUS ORDERS IN ENGLAND, vol. II, p. 101.
49. THE LIVES OF JOHN WYCLIF AND OF THE MOST EMINENT OF HIS DISCIPLES, pp. 15-16.
50. SELECT ENGLISH WORKS, Ed. T. Arnold, vol. III, p. 278.
51. *De Oratione*, ch. 4, POLEMICAL WORKS, I, 349. Quoted by David Knowles, op. cit., p. 101.
52. SELECT ENGLISH WORKS, vol. II, p. 30.
53. Ibid., III, 335.
54. Ibid., II, 257.
55. Ibid., III, 367, 372, 373, 375, 387.
56. *Fasciculi Zizaniorum*, p. 55.
57. INTRODUCTION TO POLEMICAL WORKS, R. Buddensieg, p. xx.
58. McFarlane, p. 96.
59. THE DAWN OF THE REFORMATION, vol. I, p. viii.
60. Trans. from *De Veritate Sacrae Scripturae*, by Lewis Sergeant, op. cit., p. 10.
61. *De Civili Dominio*, I, p. 358.

62. MEDIEVAL PANORAMA, G. G. Coulton, p. 488.
63. SELECT ENGLISH WORKS, vol. III, pp. 203, 228.
64. THE PEOPLE'S FAITH IN THE TIME OF WYCLIF, B. L. Manning, p. 113 f.
65. *De Blasphemia*, p. 190.
66. SELECT ENGLISH WORKS, vol. III, p. 170.

CHAPTER TWO

The Attack on the Medieval Church

THE QUESTION OF importance to be answered is whether or not Wyclif's attack on the medieval Church was justified. If it was not, and his fierce denunciations were the exaggerations of a frustrated churchman with a bad temper, then the attack was not a significant contribution to Reform. History is not changed by those who denounce evils which are the product of their own imaginations. On the other hand, if Wyclif's strong words were the sober truth, or anything like it, then his attack was part of the necessary prelude to revolutionary change. If the church in the fourteenth century was as he described it, then ruthless exposure was bound to be the first step to Reform, however negative such an exposure might seem to be. The disease had to be diagnosed before it could be cured. We shall therefore consider Wyclif's attack in its various aspects and try to determine which of these alternatives is the truth.

His attack upon the Papacy deserves attention; for what we find in his writings is not an occasional denunciation of some papal abuse but a frontal attack upon the institution, together with some indications, usually implicit rather than explicit, of a possible alternative. Two convictions of Wyclif are relevant to this attack. One is his acceptance of Scripture as the final authority in all matters of faith and practice. Again and again he contrasted the institution of the Papacy with the life of the apostles as recorded in the Bible. The temporal power of the Pope was, as Marsiglio had said in *Defensor Pacis*, unscriptural, and the primacy of Peter in the New Testament was not in worldly dignity, might and

renown, but in faith, humility and meekness. Christ Himself
had no temporal power. "It is plain that no man should be
Pope unless he is a son of Christ and of Peter, imitating them
in deeds".[1] The other conviction is that of the supremacy of
the first three centuries of the Church and the thoroughly
retrograde step taken by Constantine in endowing the Church
and of Sylvester in accepting the endowment. This injected
the poison of temporal power into the bloodstream of the
Church. Wyclif agreed with Dante:

> Ah Constantine! What ills were gendered there
> No, not from thy conversion, but the dower
> The first rich Pope received from thee as heir[2];

and with the author of the pseudo-Joachim commentary on
Jeremiah who labelled Sylvester "the first rich Father".

Such positive notions of the Papacy as Wyclif had stemmed
from these convictions. He insisted on poverty and virtue as
the only proper states for one who claimed to be the Vicar of
Christ. Those who sat in St. Peter's chair should be, like him,
without gold or silver. Their lives should be "of the greatest
possible virtue and in conversation, like Christ".[3] The "Bible
Papacy" consisted in a poor and humble life, spent in the
service of the Church, setting before God's people an example
of Christian goodness. The Pope must be the shepherd of the
flock and the preacher who brought men to Christ. This was
the true Papacy that had to be distinguished from the false;
and the more clear the idea became in Wyclif's mind the
more virulent became his attack upon those who, in his
judgment, fell short of it.

He attacked strongly the temporal power of the Pope. He
condemned the papal pretence that love of temporal power
proceeded from charity and zeal for the Church's rights and
urged that "for the destruction of this papal error the whole
of Christendom and particularly the bishops, ought to rise
up".[4] The conception of the Papacy as a political power
striving for the mastery by political means was anathema
to him. This made him detest the trappings of power and he
fulminated against the worldliness and luxury of both Rome

and Avignon. He echoed the words of Arnold of Brescia earlier in the Middle Ages that the Pope's "sole concern was to glut his appetite and to fill his coffers by draining those of others".[5] He asked the simple, penetrating question, "Lord, if Christ would not have as much as a little house in which to rest his head, as peculiarly his own, how should Christ's vicar be so great a lord in this world?"[6] He particularly resented the fact that one of the sources of this opulence was England and he heartily disliked those methods of financial extortion at which the Papacy was so expert. The claims of Gregory XI to the sovereignty and wealth of England Wyclif dismissed as *deliramenta*, and he pointed out very firmly, in answer to a request from Parliament, that the Pope was only entitled to gifts of charity and that money needed so badly at home should not be sent abroad.

There was one sense in which Wyclif welcomed the Great Schism of 1378. The spectacle of two rival Popes excommunicating each other seemed to him to be a confirmation for all to see of the spiritual bankruptcy of the office and the need to put something else in its place. "Many noble, catholic truths are made plain by this happy division".[7] There is some hesitancy in Wyclif's views at this point. In *De Potestate Papae* he first of all wrote that the Church would be better off without the rival Popes and suggested, as Michael of Casena had done earlier in the century, that the old method of government by Council should be resuscitated,[8] but later began a chapter by assuming the necessity of one Pope and discussing the limits of his authority.[9] All he appeared to be sure of was that anything was preferable to such a monstrous division of Christendom, for "this happy division" was only a debating point. The real effect of the Schism upon him was one of revulsion. Though he preferred the English choice, Urban VI, to Gregory XI (whom he referred to in *De Ecclesia* as *horrendus dyabolus*), he said that the two of them were like dogs snarling over a bone. Looking at the two rival claimants in their quarrel he asked the question, "Can we possibly believe that the Pope, in his own

31

person, keeps the commands which Christ gave to the apostles?"[10]

Wyclif's view hardened later into a belief that the Pope was Antichrist and if there were two of them they shared that unholy designation. At first, as J. P. Whitney points out,[11] to be Antichrist was a "phase of character" rather than "a personal existence", but Wyclif finally came to believe that the Pope was "consistently and always Antichrist". His theology of salvation was predestinarian and included the belief that nobody knows whether a given Pope (or anybody else) belongs to the true Church. There was therefore no reason why he should not be Antichrist. On this uncomplimentary theme Wyclif expatiated. In *De Potestate Papae* he described the eleven characteristics of Antichrist[12] and the point of them all was to show how far the Papacy had departed from the simple faith and practice of Christ and His disciples. Because of this the Pope "works for the cause of the devil against Christ".[13] Antichrist is in one place and another described as arrogant, puffed up with worldly glory, a hypocrite, a seducer, an apostate and an inveterate adversary of Christ. In the last five chapters of *De Christo et suo adversario* Wyclif demonstrated in twelve cases the proposition that the Pope stood in a position of total antagonism to Christ, and again the contrast was between the Papacy of the fourteenth century with its riches and power and the simple life of the New Testament. Here the strong language of Wyclif came into its own . . . "the prince of liars", "a most arrogant man, and cruelly vindictive", "the Pope is always provoking wars", "unquestionably satanic and dyabolic", "against Jesus Christ".[14]

Most of Wyclif's criticisms are just enough. When due allowance has been made for the redeeming features of the various Popes and the highly coloured rhetoric of our author we are left with a mass of evidence which substantiates Wyclif's point of view.

Wyclif was right in accusing the Papacy of a love of temporal power. The long era in which it had stood for unity, centralization and the pre-eminence of morality over the law of the jungle had by the fourteenth century come to an end and the Pope was rapidly becoming one power among others. The struggle for supremacy amongst the rising nations had begun and most of the Popes fell for the temptation of joining in. Crusading armies were raised to fight for the papal cause and in struggles like those against Naples and Florence the Pope was seen, not in his old role of spiritual sovereign, but as a temporal power plotting and fighting against his enemies, with lands and gold as the prize.

It is not surprising that in this new situation the Papacy did everything possible to increase its power and authority in the now separate nations. One such effort was the continued imposition of that legal system which made the *Curia* the supreme court of appeal for all Christendom. Both first cases and appeals of every conceivable kind were supposed to be sent to Rome or Avignon for settlement. The roads to the papal cities were crammed with litigants and the lawyers were burdened far beyond their capacity. Ignoring the accusations of bribery and corruption, one can hardly believe that the purpose of all this legal traffic was the disinterested pursuit of justice. Efficiency called for some form of decentralization, but that would have weakened the papal power to the benefit of the nations and consequently attempts to bring it about, like the Statutes of Praemunire in England, were resisted.

The Holy See did its best to maintain a financial grip upon every country and against these acts of extortion the protests of Wyclif were fully justified. The most famous is the case of "provisions", made such a powerful and lucrative asset by the Bulls *Ex debito* and *Execrabilis* of John XXII. That there were some advantages in the Pope "providing" benefices in every country is undeniable. It meant that the see or benefice did not remain vacant and forgotten for years on end (though other systems could have had the same effect), and it prevented the parochial wrangles and misguided choices which are inevitable in matters dealt with at a local level. From the point of view of the King and other collators the system was not unattractive, for an arrangement could often be made by which the Pope accepted their nomination and then proceeded to make money for himself on the mandate for the provision; the result being what A. H. Thompson calls "the habitual collusion between the Crown and the Papacy in the matter of provisions".[15] Through this system the Papacy centralized control and extracted money. Foreigners at Rome and Avignon drew the money from English benefices, for they, with their easy access to the papal court, were the first to hear of the vacancies.[16] Meanwhile, in the sees and parishes concerned, the churches fell into disrepair and the hungry sheep looked up and were not fed. Many cardinals, for example, held livings in England and it seems likely that money collected from their sinecures went from their coffers at Avignon to support French arms against the English. After persistent demands from people and Parliament an attempt was made to remedy the situation by the Statute of Provisors (1351), but lacking the wholehearted support of the King, it was largely ineffectual and subsequent attempts produced only slight improvement.

Considerable sums of money were involved in this system. There were the fees, amounting to one-third of a year's income, payable by bishops or abbots who were appointed to their offices by the Pope, and further fees on receiving the *pallium*; there was a tax of one-tenth of the net income of every benefice to which the Pope appointed; there were the annates, defined by W. E. Lunt[17] as "a portion of the first year's revenues of a benefice paid to the Pope on the occasion of a new collation, provided the benefice did not pay services"; and there was the income from the papal benefices which were left, sometimes deliberately, vacant. These taxes were not manumitted and every incumbent was responsible for the debts of his predecessors. To this regular system of extortion must be added periodic demands of a special kind, as when in 1365 Urban V asked for the one thousand marks promised annually by King John, or when in 1363 Gregory XI demanded a hundred thousand florins from the English clergy to carry on his war against Milan. The whole system of papal taxation was a grievous burden in

England, and although not every Pope had the rapacity of a Boniface IX not one of them was able or willing to abolish or to reform drastically the iniquitous system.

It is understandable that with such an income the Popes should find it impossible to resist temptations to worldliness and luxury. Even before the Bulls of John XXII the *Libere de Flore*[18] suggested that the robbery of the papal treasury at Anagni was a proof of God's hatred of the worldliness and luxury of the Church, though it must be conceded that the author was not unbiased. A Roman Catholic author calls it "the sacrilege of Agnani".[19] Most historians turn naturally to Avignon to substantiate the thesis and although some good came from the Papacy there—an administrative reorganization, certain reforms in the Monastic Orders and a commendable if spasmodic enthusiasm for missionary work are examples—the overall picture is of a life of worldly splendour and magnificence. The Popes at Avignon had what Guillaume Mollat calls "a vast fiscal system designed to secure to them considerable pecuniary resources".[20] Retinues, often running into hundreds of relatives and parasites of various kinds, gathered around most of the prominent officers, all of them only too happy to share in the luxurious life of the papal court. Doubtless the corruptions of *la peccherouse cité d'Avenon* have been exaggerated by Petrarch, Boccaccio and other critics, and some Popes, like Benedict XII, were better than others; but the general impression given by the papal court at Avignon is one of the evils attendant upon love of power and money. Elliott-Binns gives a sound judgment: "During the papal residence Avignon obtained a most unenviable reputation; but there are reasons for supposing that *although this condemnatory opinion was justified* [my italics] it was also exaggerated".[21]

The Great Schism of 1378, the immediate cause of which was a legal wrangle, is impossible to defend and deserves all the strictures passed upon it by Wyclif. Clement VII and Urban VI split Christendom in two and by this divisive act the spiritual power of the Church was undermined in every land. National quarrels were made more bitter,

35

military exploits like the foolish and abortive crusade of the Bishop of Norwich in 1383 were undertaken in the name of rival claimants, the religious orders joined in the controversy and faithful Christians everywhere were horrified to contemplate the division of the indivisible. This sorry state lasted for nearly forty years and even led to three Popes instead of two before the Conciliar Movement did its best to repair the ruins.

As far as the accusation of Antichrist is concerned the most one can establish is the evil characteristics of some Popes. When one considers the political manoeuvres of Boniface III, the avarice of John XXII (twenty-five million gold crowns in coin and jewels were found in the papal treasury at his death—the Spiritual Franciscans called him Antichrist) and Clement VI, the stubborn recklessness and incorrigible arrogance of Urban VI (here perhaps Wyclif's judgment was led astray by his nationalist sentiments, but in the direction of too much charity!), and the greed of Boniface IX, one can appreciate how tempted Wyclif was to sum up such satanic traits, as the Béguins had done before him, in the one appropriate noun. Taken in its full literal sense the word is an exaggeration, for it introduces a theological concept into what should be strictly an attack upon morals. Again, Wyclif did not always distinguish clearly between the office of the Pope and the moral stature of the particular person who held it; and to argue, as he did, from the sad state of the latter that the former was evil was not the best of logic. But on the question of the moral and spiritual qualities, or lack of them, of the various Popes, though his language may have been extreme his charges were never without substance. The enemy he fought was not a figment of his imagination.

A similar conclusion can be drawn from Wyclif's attacks upon other sections of the medieval Church. Beneath his polemical language lie inescapable facts. He spoke strongly about those whom he labelled "Caesarean clergy". "No man is honourable who joins together the peculiar value and authority of the clerical office with the value and authority of the lay office".[22] Such a connection was "inexcusable" and "blasphemous". The substance of Wyclif's charge was, that an office under the Crown which would be honourable to a layman (his patriotism would not allow him to deny this) became a disgrace when joined by an ecclesiastic to his other work, since he then neglected his true calling for a lower one. Such a person was "a deceitful man bringing pollution into his glorious soul".[23] In *De Quattuor Sectis Novellis* the *clerus cesareus* are the First Sect and Wyclif condemned them for trying to possess what by right belonged to the temporal power. In *De Blasphemia* he wrote, with Sudbury in his mind, "How, I ask, does it belong to an archbishop to seize that prerogative of a king which is the most secular part of the king's office?",[24] and he went on to describe such a prelate as a traitor to the King, the kingdom and God, who ruined the first two and grievously offended the third.

Wyclif's arrows, though barbed, were not far wide of the mark. Ubertino da Casale and Arnold of Catalonia had written of the worldliness and financial preoccupations of the Italian and French prelates seventy years before and the habit had spread since then. The English bench of bishops in the fourteenth century, men like Wykeham, Courtenay, Spenser and Sudbury, were shrewd persons of affairs who gave much time to secular business. They organized the diplomatic, administrative and financial affairs of the State and did it more efficiently than anyone else could, but at a considerable cost to the spiritual work of their dioceses. The bishop was often much more the eminent civil servant than he was the *pastor pastorum*. Out of twenty-five persons who were bishops in England and Wales between 1376 and 1386 thirteen held high secular offices in the King's service and some of the others had their fingers in various political pies. This meant that in many dioceses clergy were idle or corrupt, buildings fell into disrepair and ordinations and confirmations went by default because of the inadequacy or complete lack of episcopal oversight and visitation. The bishops were not alone in these practices and both cardinals and parish priests were to be found in the service of the

State, much to the impoverishment of the Church. "The Crown sought for and found its most competent ministers among the bishops and the clergy".[25] If, as W. A. Pantin argues,[26] "this entanglement and exploitation" (and Pantin believes that in this matter the Church was the exploited and not the exploiter) "was part of a price paid for a noble conception of Christian society in which Church and State were interwoven and identified", then the price was too high. Wyclif was right in this matter, though in his zeal he tended to overlook those who continued faithfully in the work to which they were ordained.

Wyclif also attacked the monks in their monasteries, though not with the same blistering invective which he used on other sections of the Church. This is significant, for in a critic as destructive as Wyclif what is not said is as important as what is. In *De Blasphemia* he criticized them for their possession of property, a matter which always riled him because he believed it to be so unlike the Church of the New Testament. He pointed his accusing finger at the immense wealth which lay idle in their monasteries. Monks had the character of useless parasites, a charge he illustrated with a botanical reference to plants that sucked juices from the earth in summer but always returned them as dead leaf manure in the autumn.[27] They were the Second Sect in *De Quattuor* and there again the two charges were possession of property and general uselessness. If the Monastic Orders were abolished large sums of money would become available for the poor; consequently he believed that they "shulden ceese bi Christis lawe". His works contain a few harmless gastronomic references ("thei asken largeness of flesche and of fische"), but there is no torrent of abuse poured upon their heads.

His judgment in their case seems sound enough. There were positive virtues in the monastic system, like the regular offering of worship and prayer, the distribution of alms, the tradition of hospitality ("the cooking and accommodation in monasteries were far superior to those that could be got in inns"[28]), the hard work of sheep-farming, the preservation of

38

books and manuscripts, the compilation of chronicles (not all of them unbiased!) of which Wyclif may well have been aware. What one student of the period[29] calls "the established works of piety" were not unknown to him. At the same time his criticisms must stand. Some of the monasteries did possess great wealth. As J. C. Dickinson says: "Wealth . . . was most unevenly distributed, and many houses were far from affluent, but the aggregate of English monastic wealth was now very considerable".[30] The abbey churches were some of the greatest in size and in the wealthier houses paid servants considerably outnumbered the brethren. To quote Dom David Knowles, "In 1292 [at Durham] the bursar's receipts were £3,741, and in 1308 £4,526. These *huge totals* [my italics] included the revenues of both cellarer and master of the garner".[31] The contemporary *Dives and Pauper* refers to "these men of Holy Church . . . monks and chanones that . . . ride on high horses with saddles harnessed with gold and silver more pompously than Lords".[32] Living was high because the accrued wealth of innumerable endowments was there to be spent. Dom David Knowles refers to the characteristics of Chaucer's Monk—"expensive dress, love of good cheer, rejection of austerity and appeals to the Rule, and above all a love of hunting",[33] and says that these are "faults all but endemic in the monastic body". It is true also that, apart from the virtues already mentioned, and they were by no means universal, the monks were generally useless to the community. Often with nothing better to do, they fell to quarrelling amongst themselves, and mismanagement and laxity were common features in the episcopal reports when they were made. But the wild excesses in which critics of monasticism so easily indulge are not borne out by the facts, nor do they appear in the criticisms of Wyclif. His more moderate attack was justified.

The friars were treated very differently. Towards the ideals of their movement Wyclif was not unsympathetic. He believed in the virtue of poverty and had considerable affinities with the Spiritual Franciscans who opposed strongly, even fanatically, the materialism which had invaded their Order. One can see in his Poor Priests that the ideal of the true mendicant was dear to him and, as is not unusual, the corruption of a cherished ideal aroused more hostility than movements, like the monastic, which were basically alien to his spirit. But even this was, with Wyclif, a slow process. At first, sympathy with the ideal and no doubt Christian charity (despite all his critics have said Wyclif did not attack people just for the love of doing it) made him reasonably tolerant towards the friars, and Lingard's picture of a man who hated them right from the start[34] is overdrawn. He recognized their occasional usefulness: "it occurs that some men are improved by submitting to these disciplines, that otherwise would be wild",[35] admitted that there were "many holy and serious priests"[36] among them and even went so far as to call some of them *filios karissimos*.[37] He was not averse to having them as his allies in making a case against the *possessionati* or "Caesarean clergy" as he called them, and no doubt he was delighted when two Austin Friars presented formal articles to Parliament in 1371 pleading for a partial confiscation of the Church's wealth. At the instigation of John of Gaunt four friars came to Wyclif's defence at the abortive trial in St. Paul's in 1377, and he acknowledged this help graciously: ". . . who stood by my side fearlessly in the cause of God".[38] He must have been aware too of their intellectual standing at Oxford and have thoroughly approved of their insistence on Bible study there. A number of factors, however, were responsible for a deterioration in Wyclif's relations with them.

One was his conviction that they were a "sect", one of what he called in *Trialogus* the *religiones privatae*, and he denounced them as such in *De Quattuor* where they appear as the Fourth Sect. His charge against them was that they divided the Body of Christ. He appealed to the New Testament revelation: "Christ did not institute these sects for the edification of the Church . . . they have no foundation in our Lord Jesus Christ".[39] Nothing could be further from our Lord's prayer that His Church might be one than these divisive Orders. "Men may openly say how friars reckon more by their new Order and their ordinance than they do by Christ's law or profit of His Church".[40]

Wyclif did not like the friars functioning as the Pope's "private army". He resented the fact that they were "exempt from bischopis and other ordinaries" and gave their first loyalty to the "bischop of Rome", and this resentment increased as his attitude to the Papacy hardened. He complained that "They are not lawful men under the King of the land . . . they are immediately under the Pope and are not subject to the bishop of any temporal lord".[41] He thoroughly disapproved of their refusal to pay taxes. A "state within a state" of this kind was offensive to one with his nationalistic conception of the Church.

The wealth and property amassed by the friars Wyclif roundly condemned. In *De Triplici Vinculo Amoris*[42] he wrote of their "fantastic expenditure", their "sumptuous buildings", and stated that these cost the English realm the sum of £40,000 every year. Again in *De Apostasia* he complained, "They are said to have regal palaces, houses and churches, excessive in size, in subtlety, in costliness and with glittering ornaments for decoration".[43] He repeated the charge in English—they "have overmuch wealth, both in great wasteful houses, in precious clothes, in great feasts and many jewels and treasures".[44] This seemed to him to be totally unscriptural, "dampned by God, bothe in the Olde Testament and in the New". It was a sin which corrupted the friars themselves, left the genuine poor without succour and impoverished the whole community. The fact that it arose through begging and the soliciting of endowments angered Wyclif the more.

He further contended that the friars were a menace to the spiritual work of the parish. They presumed to hear confessions and to absolve from sin, but for the sake of financial gain sat lightly upon their responsibilities. "Also these new religious, and specifically the friars . . . through private confession they nourish much sin, namely lechery, adultery and sins against nature, extortion and robbery and usury, to participate in them, and tell not the truth in confession for fear of both losing friendship and establishing and maintaining their false Order".[45] The spiritual damage done was considerable, for the sinners who confessed to a begging friar "forsake their own curates who would warn them of the perils"[46] and so the friars "make dissension between curates and their spiritual children".[47] Wyclif, who was nothing if not serious, did not approve of the light and popular preaching with which the friars titivated the people, and referred to it as "cronyclis and fablis to pleese the puple".[48] "They do not preach the word of God in sincerity", he wrote in *De Ordinatione Fratrum*.[49] In *De Officio Pastorali* he went further and called them "adulterers of the Word of God in prostitutes' robes and coloured veils".[50]

These factors were responsible for an ever widening gulf between Wyclif and the friars, but what made it quite unbridgeable was the fact that when he proclaimed his novel views on the Eucharist they immediately set themselves up as the champions of Catholic orthodoxy. In this controversy Wyclif lost most of his old friends, like Thomas Winterton who had admired him for years but who now responded to the *Confessio*, in which Wyclif's views on the Eucharist were stated, with his own *Absolutio* in which he said that he now saw "with tearful eyes the many errors and heresies that are contained in a certain *Confessio* of a most famous doctor". The Blackfriars Synod of 1382 which pronounced Wyclif's doctrine of the Eucharist "heretical" was called by him, not without reason, "this counseil of freris", and the opposition at Oxford was led by a Carmelite Friar, Peter Stokes. Wyclif retaliated fiercely and in his *Fifty Heresies and Errors of Friars* he spoke his mind. He called them "Caymes Castels", an abusive acrostic term;[51] described them as "hated and cursid of God Almighty", "ypocrisie", "ghostly synne of Sodome", and the like. On the specific question of the Eucharist he accused them in return of bringing in a "new heresie" which denied that the bread was really Christ's Body but was instead "accident withouten suggett [subject] or noght".[52] This he maintained was a denial of "holy writt".

42

Were Wyclif's facts right and his judgments sound? Again we find ourselves having to make allowances for exaggerated language, particularly in the later English tracts. In the heat of the battle he said things which in calmer moments he would certainly have wished to qualify or retract. One example is mentioned by Workman[53] who can hardly be accused of not giving Wyclif his due. In his *Controversial Tracts* Wyclif quoted against the friars that twelfth-century controversialist Hildegard of Bringen, of whom Charles Singer[54] says with some insight, "Hers was a fiery, a prophetic, in many ways a singularly noble spirit, but she was not a saint in any intelligible sense of the word". In *De Blasphemia, Contra Fratres*[55] Wyclif wrote: "Also Hildegard says that these cursed sects shall be destroyed and damned in hell", and though this critical prophetess undoubtedly poured out her scorn upon the corrupt clergy, her dates (1098-1179) preclude the words quoted from being a direct reference to the friars. Wyclif was so anxious to turn his guns on his enemies that he was not always careful to examine closely his ammunition.

Despite this now familiar fault the truth is that the evils which Wyclif attacked were real evils. Corroboration of this comes from many quarters and one or two examples must suffice, but before noticing them it should be remembered in mitigation that the friar was an easy enemy. He represented an ideal so lofty that hypocrisy was inevitable; he worked not in the secret of the cloister but in the open where all his faults were visible; he was a bird of passage and as such inevitably drew from the more static members of the community some criticisms which can be put down to defence mechanisms covering their own deficiencies. Nor were all friars deserving of the fierce attacks launched upon the Orders as a whole. The Word of God was in some places faithfully proclaimed and excellent pastoral work was done, but when all this has been considered there remains more than enough evidence to justify the general position of Wyclif.

That the friars were a divisive "sect" can hardly be denied

when one thinks of the controversies with the seculars over the intrusion into diocesan and parochial organization and the theological and legal arguments between bishops and friars which they involved. Then there was considerable strife in the Church over the question of poverty, of which the friars made so much, and the story of the struggles between the Conventual and Zealot parties of the Franciscan Order would take a long time to tell. As Dom David Knowles points out,[56] on the essence of the virtue of poverty the Minors were opposed by the Dominicans and other friars; on the lawfulness of mendicancy the friars were opposed by the seculars; on the absolute value of material poverty the Spiritual Franciscans were opposed by everybody else. The controversy was sharp and there was abuse in plenty. The pseudo-Joachim commentary on Jeremiah compared the Dominican Order to a crow and the Franciscan to a dove. William Langland was very conscious of the competition and strife between "freres of alle fyve ordres" and thought that they offended the principle "for alle we ben brethren thauh we be diursliche clothede".[57] Not infrequently the growth and prosperity of the particular Order was of more concern than the peace of the Church.

The friars were indeed the Pope's "private army", for by the Bull *Super cathedram* of Boniface VII (reaffirmed by the decretal *Dudum* of Clement V in 1312) the friars were given the right to work in the secular dioceses as preachers and confessors and in 1321 John XXII gave them full authority to exercise any sacerdotal function in any parish. As Baskerville says, "The friars were almost wholly free from episcopal interference". [58] Naturally enough, in the face of local resentment they turned to the source of their privileges and rights and gave their loyalty to the Papacy, an arrangement which was by no means unfavourable to the latter. H. B. Workman says they became "Rome's network of irresponsible police".[59]

The charge that the friars had too much wealth and property was put forcibly by Richard Fitzralph, Archbishop of Armagh. They were mercenary in their motives when they heard confessions and as a result they amassed considerable wealth. "After the friars had obtained the privilege of hearing confessions, they built beautiful monasteries and regal palaces as though they were for kings".[60] That such monies might have been given to the local parish church adds bitterness to the charge. Fitzralph objected strongly to this accumulation of wealth through beggary. "I reckon that since the world was first made there never was an easier way, more sly and cunning, to accumulate riches than by the aforesaid privileges with the obligation of beggary".[61] Langland repeated the charge and constantly accused the friars of working "for moneye". So with irony and geniality did Chaucer:

> Therefore in stede of wepynge and preyeres
> Men moote yeve silver to the povre freres[62]

though he was not as "povre" as he liked to pretend:

> But he was lyk a maister or a pope
> Of double worstede was his semycope.[63]

Chaucer corroborates too the accusation of spending money on ecclesiastical buildings. The Friar of Holderness at the opening of the *Somnour's Tale* asks people:

> to yeve, for Goddes sake,
> Wherewith men myghte hooly houses make.[64]

At the beginning of the fourteenth century the Franciscan, Ubertino da Casale, had complained bitterly about the luxurious buildings of his own Order in Italy. As Decima Douie says, "His [Ubertino's] description of the stable at Bethlehem gives rise to a fierce invective against the sumptuous convents which were springing up in so many of the Italian towns, rivalling in their architecture the palaces of princes and great nobles",[65] and M. D. Lambert adds the comment: "His [Ubertino's] views were supported by less biased authorities. Much earlier Pecham, who shared the standards of his master Bonaventura, had called these over-large buildings *'monstra professionis'*."[66] Many similar

45

protests are to be found in the writings of the Fraticelli. William of St. Armour said that the friars were worse than the devil; the devil proposed to turn stones into bread; the friars turn the bread of the poor into stones.[67] According to A. G. Little the great building programme began in England about 1270 and lasted some fifty years.[68]

Writing from his own pastoral experience, Fitzralph substantiates the charge that the smooth and effective spiritual work of the parish was menaced by the intrusion of the friars. He believed that, "for parishioners of any church to shrive themselves only to one person, the ordinary is more worthy to be chosen than any friar".[69] It was far better, he argued, to deal with the man who had known them from infancy. The friars he found quite unscrupulous. They incite people not to pay their tithes and "appropriate such offerings to their own use".[70] He accused them of having sexual relationships with the women of the parish, though this is not a charge made much of by Wyclif. William Langland supplies further evidence of the interference of friars in parish work where they went "for profit and for helthe and for to seke festes". The charge of immorality is repeated (as it is in the *Confessio Amantis* of John Gower where a passage on "Love-Drunkenness" is introduced by the words, "or elles as a lewed Frere")[71] and the friar dubbed *"Sire Penetrans-domos"*. Again, the "parsons and parish priests that should the people shrive" were frustrated in their work by those who "flee to the friars".[72] This served only to cause trouble in the parish, "for they hear parsons shrive without licence and leave and this fosters anger. As a result they so speak and dispute that each despises the other".[73] The masterly sketch of the Friar in Chaucer's Prologue shows that Wyclif was not condemning the friars' activities without reason:

> Ful swetely herde he confessioun
> And plesaunt was his absolucioun[74].

There is evidence too that some of their sermons were as Wyclif described them, for as Beryl Smalley says,[75] "The desire for novelty in his audience pushes the preacher ever further afield. Men prefer a story from the Fathers to one from Scripture and a tale from a chronicler or a pagan writer to either." "So he [the friar preacher] spreads truth and fiction about the ancients indiscriminately in such a way as to give pleasure".[76] G. R. Owst gives his own charitable interpretation of this. "Of the Mendicants perhaps we may say that their view of popular instruction was sometimes wide enough to include these things ['scattered, garbled excerpts from classical sources'] as valuable for their own sake to the ordinary man."[77] But all this is some distance removed from H. B. Workman's description of the first Franciscan preachers—"men preaching Christ with burning love and conviction".[78]

As far as the attack on the friars' eucharistic position is concerned, unquestionably they maintained the orthodox doctrine of Transubstantiation and would have none of Wyclif's novel ideas, though no judgment can here be made against them without prejudging theological questions to which we must turn our attention later.

The case against the friars is admirably summed up by Dom David Knowles, who can scarcely be charged with prejudice against the religious. "The close agreement between Langland, Wyclif and Chaucer as to the worldliness of the monks and the rascality of the friars is too remarkable to be dismissed. It is, we may feel, only a partial picture . . . Nevertheless it is hard to escape the conviction that the three writers . . . are in their different ways witnesses to a corruption among the Mendicants and a worldliness among the black monks which were only too real, whatever limits we may put upon their extent and the severity of their incidence".[79] Substantially, Wyclif was right.

The final phase of Wyclif's attack on the medieval Church which we shall consider is his opposition to some of the popular religious practices of his time. He attacked, for example, the practice of excommunication and, as with so many of his subjects, he grew more severe with the passage of time. At first he was content to make observations with

47

which no one could quarrel. Excommunication was unjust if it was imposed "out of rancour or in a vindictive spirit" or "for temporal gain" or if it was undeserved.[80] Unjust excommunication was worse than murder. He was not happy about the rules governing relations with excommunicated persons and he would not allow prelates to put them in prison. All this was reasonable enough, but later his opposition became more radical and his language fiercer. The wicked clergy must be the first to be cast out and he contended "that prelates that are so ready to curse should not sit on God's right hand, but on his left hand in hell".[81] The Christian was instructed, "Dread thou not such cursings" and excommunication was referred to as "man's curse". When he saw it as a possible hindrance to his cherished scheme of disendowment he grew more heated still. If "worldly clerks" contended that "the king and lords may not amend the clergy and turn their temporalities into secular men's hands, for fear of the curse", then "say that they babble of Antichrist's curse . . . but they speak not of the curse of God".[82]

In the main this seems a sound enough judgment. Excommunication was used against every invader of ecclesiastical privileges and temporalities and instead of being the ultimate deterrent of the Church it had become the sword which the clergy flourished at even the smallest alarum. It was, for example, the duty of the priest to excommunicate those who defrauded the Church of tithes, and one of the virtues of Chaucer's Parson of the Town was that he was "full loth to cursen for his tithes". Wyclif was hasty in condemnation when he saw excommunication as a possible obstacle to disendowment, but as this was his panacea for most of the ills of the medieval Church, his attitude can be understood. For the most part his protests were valid. Excommunications had become altogether too indiscriminate. They were, as one historian puts it, "licensed even for a schoolmaster to curb unruly boys".

Wyclif's attitude to the organized worship of the Church was, as we have noticed, puritanical,[83] but his attack upon it was, on the whole, restrained. For theological reasons he was severe on the Mass[84] but for the rest he was content to state without invective his own austere point of view. He insisted that ritual must have a spiritual significance. "Would that such ceremonies and rituals were not multiplied in our Church for then the *facta sanctorum* and other rites are not praiseworthy nor do they lift the spirit to the love of the Lord Jesus Christ".[85] Wyclif disapproved of loud singing and intoning which he called "grete criynge and blowynge of mannus vois",[86] and preferred the devout and silent prayer of our Lord and His apostles. "Not with a loud voice should we pray to God but with a much desired silence".[87] In his comments on church music he laid bare the danger in all ritual. Quoting Augustine, he wrote: "As often as the song delighteth me more than that which is sung, so often I acknowledge that I trespass grievously".[88] What priests should do is "not chant nor sing but read the gospel."

He had the same austere approach to church architecture and decoration and was also dubious about the value of the festivals of the Church, being afraid that men would love them more than they loved their Lord. The worship of images he denounced: "All men worshipping in any way those images and paintings sin and commit idolatry",[89] but because he realized that images rightly used could help devotion he advocated no iconoclastic attempt to remove them from the churches. So with the saints. He abhorred saint-worship and because they led in that direction he felt that individual honours paid to saints were dangerous. Canonization by Rome, he later came to believe, was no guarantee that a man was even *membrum ecclesiae triumphantis*, but he did not wish to eliminate the saints from the life of the Church and he had no objection to a general trust in their prayers. The same moderation can be seen in his attitude to the Virgin Mary. She was "blessid in hevene", "withouten synne", and from that celestial abode "Marie help the Chirche". She was to be reverenced, for "Jesus and Mary are the cause of man's salvation",[90] and she was "the chaumbre of his manhood". He commended the "fyve festis of our Ladi" including the Assumption. Though he did not advocate praying to her there was no Protestant rancour in his attitude, a deficiency which was made good by his followers.

Whilst we may not share Wyclif's puritanical taste in church music, ritual and decoration, we can appreciate his passion for sincerity in worship. At the end of the fourteenth century the Latin in which the Mass was celebrated was unintelligible to most ordinary people and the symbolism of worship had become a science which only the learned could appreciate. In those circumstances a plea that worship should always "lift the spirit to the love of the Lord Jesus Christ" was no bad thing. In an age when markets were sometimes held inside the church, when young lovers did their wooing during the most solemn moments of the Mass and when Bishop Grandisson could complain of vicars choral calling out loudly to the officiating priest to speed-up his ministrations, a word spoken for reverence, simplicity, and reality in worship was not out of place. Both Gower and the author of *Dives and Pauper* testify to the fact that people did worship images and Wyclif was right to condemn the practice. He was right too not to demand the removal of all images, for, as the author of *Festial* has it, "there are many thousands of people who could not imagine in their hearts how Christ was crucified unless they had learned it from the sight of images and paintings".[91] Similarly with the saints and the Virgin Mary. It is impossible to quarrel with the moderate Wyclif and one is left wondering whether or not his protest would have been more effective in the long run if this moderation had pervaded all his works and been more marked in his Lollard following.

Wyclif was no lover of indulgences. He rejected the notion of a store-house of merit at the disposal of the Pope on which the indulgence theory rested. "This false fantasy of spiritual treasure in heaven, that each Pope is made dispenser of this treasure at his own will, this is a facile word imagined without ground".[92] God alone, he argued in *De Ecclesia*, could remit sin and "he had not left in his law this power to the Pope".[93] As he explained in one of his Controversial Tracts, "As if the Pope could grant the good will of Christ! That is good will before the Pope grant it".[94] To ignore this leads to the intolerable position where the Pope is "lord of Crist". The fact that papal indulgences were sold for money drew forth some scathing comments from Wyclif. Could God sell righteousness? The idea was ludicrous. But it became diabolically wicked when the selling was done by the Pope for his own worldly ends. Nothing horrified him more than the sale of indulgences by one Pope to raise funds to fight against the other. That was "an open blasphemy that men should horror for to hear".[95]

Leaving the theological question on one side for the moment, the abuses in practice of the indulgence system were undeniable. As Chancellor Gascoigne complained in 1450, "Sinners say nowadays, 'I care not what or how many evils I do before God, for I can get at once, without the least difficulty, plenary remission of any guilt or sin whatsoever through an Indulgence granted me through the Pope' ".[96] The English bishops were by no means free from blame and in 1348 the Bishop of Bath and Wells promised an indulgence of forty days to all who should give alms or fast or pray to avert God's anger in sending the plague, whilst in 1396 indulgences were sold in the diocese of York to raise money for building the cathedral. Wyclif was right in contending that indulgences sank to their lowest level when the Pope presumed to sell the superabundant graces of the saints to raise funds for the crusades of the Papacy. This happened in 1383 when Spenser was organizing his ill-fated crusade on behalf of Urban, and again in 1411 when John XXIII ("anti-pope") offered indulgences to all who took up arms against the King of Naples. The attitude of Wyclif was shared by Chaucer and Langland who had no kind words for the Pardoners and their unholy wares.

To examine and justify Wyclif's attacks on the other practices of the medieval Church to which he meted out criticism would be a wearisome affair. Simony, absenteeism, pluralism, patronage, preferment, auricular confession and pilgrimages all received his attention, but what has been said of those we have examined is true of these also. His accusations were substantially true.

In summing up his whole attack on the medieval Church it must be remembered that he was not presenting, nor did he claim to present, a comprehensive picture of the Church's life and work. Unquestionably there was much that was good in the Church of the fourteenth century; some preaching was informed and effective; some friars did valuable pastoral work; some clergy tried to reduce the amount of superstition which had accumulated around the means of grace; there were honest attempts in the parishes to teach Christian morality; there was some disinterested charity and almsgiving; there were even some Popes who did not qualify for the vituperation with which Wyclif attacked their office. All this Wyclif must have known and would not, one believes, in his cooler moments wish to deny. The point is that he was not engaged in writing an accurate, balanced, sober appraisal of the life of the Church in the fourteenth century; he was attacking what seemed to him to be monstrous evils. He was not an historian, but a reformer. Consequently judgment must be passed on him not according to the wholeness of the picture he gave of the Church, but according to whether or not the evils he attacked were real evils. The evidence has brought us to the conclusion that, allowing for a certain exaggeration of language, due partly to the uninhibited form of fourteenth-century controversy and partly to the irascible temperament of Wyclif himself, the evils were as he described them.

Such an attack was a necessary prelude to Reform and was no small part of Wyclif's contribution. Indeed it can be claimed that Wyclif's onslaught was so well-directed and so devastating that he saved the Reformers of the sixteenth century the trouble of doing the job themselves. Bernard Manning argued in this way about the Papacy: "In *De Potestate Papae* . . . Wyclif destroyed most of the claims of the contemporary Papacy by a consideration of dogma and history which left little for the Renaissance scholars to add".[97] In fact they did attack the Roman Church with some spirit. Erasmus in *Encomium Moriae* bitterly criticized it, whilst Luther, like Wyclif, identified the Pope with Antichrist and in his open letter to Pope Leo X of 1520 he called the Papacy "this pestilential see", told the Pope that his throne "must seem like hell to him" and concluded: "in short all good Christians are bad Romanists".[98] But much more of this negative denunciation over a very wide field would have been necessary if Wyclif had not written as he did. As it was, he made for the Reformers the penetrating, if somewhat lurid, diagnosis of the ills of the medieval Church without which a cure was impossible. The extent to which he was able to contribute to that cure is the question to which we must now turn.

REFERENCES

1. *De Potestate Papae*, p. 215.
2. Inferno, Canto XIX, St. 115.
3. *De Potestate Papae*, p. 80.
4. Ibid., p. 300.
5. ARNOLD OF BRESCIA, G. W. Greenaway, p. 122.
6. SELECT ENGLISH WORKS, vol. II, p. 395.
7. *De Potestate Papae*, p. 353.
8. Ibid., p. 186.
9. Ibid., ch. 9.
10. POLEMICAL WORKS, vol. II. p. 60.
11. CAMBRIDGE HISTORY OF ENGLISH LITERATURE, vol. II, pp. 56-7.
12. *De Potestate Papae*, p. 120 ff.
13. *De Dissensione Paparum*, p. 573.
14. *De Christo et suo adversario*, pp. 680, 681, 687, 680, 686.
15. THE ENGLISH CLERGY AND THEIR ORGANIZATION IN THE LATER MIDDLE AGES, A. H. Thompson, p. 24.
16. Article by Miss A. Deeley, ENGLISH HISTORICAL REVIEW, vol. 43, no. 172, October 1928: "Papal Provision and Royal

Rights of Patronage in the Early Fourteenth Century",
p. 498.

17. PAPAL REVENUES IN THE MIDDLE AGES, vol. I, W. E.
Lunt, p. 93.

18. For a summary of this work see: THE NATURE AND THE
EFFECT OF THE HERESY OF THE FRATICELLI, D. L.
Douie, p. 42 ff.

19. H. K. Mann in THE LIVES OF THE POPES IN THE MIDDLE
AGES, vol. XVIII, p. 371.

20. THE POPES OF AVIGNON AND THE GREAT SCHISM: Cambridge
Medieval History, vol. VII, p. 9.

21. THE DECLINE AND FALL OF THE MEDIEVAL PAPACY,
L. E. Elliott-Binns, p. 116.

22. De Officio Regis, p. 27.

23. Ibid., p. 29.

24. De Blasphemia, p. 194.

25. THE ENGLISH CLERGY AND THEIR ORGANIZATION IN THE
LATER MIDDLE AGES, p. 15.

26. THE ENGLISH CHURCH IN THE FOURTEENTH CENTURY,
W. A. Pantin, p. 44.

27. De Blasphemia, p. 189.

28. ENGLISH MONKS AND THE SUPPRESSION OF THE MONA-
STERIES, G. Baskerville, p. 26.

29. K. L. Wood-Legh in STUDIES IN CHURCH LIFE IN ENG-
LAND UNDER EDWARD III, p. 30.

30. MONASTIC LIFE IN MEDIEVAL ENGLAND, J. C. Dickinson,
p. 86.

31. THE RELIGIOUS ORDERS IN ENGLAND, vol. II, David
Knowles, p. 317.

32. Dives and Pauper Commentary, VII, c. 12, quoted in
MEDIEVAL PANORAMA, G. G. Coulton, p. 273.

33. THE RELIGIOUS ORDERS IN ENGLAND, vol. II, p. 366.

34. HISTORY OF ENGLAND, vol. VIII, John Lingard, p. 133.

35. SELECT ENGLISH WORKS, vol. III, p. 431.

36. De Apostasia, p. 15.

37. Ibid., p. 44.

38. Ibid., p. 42.

39. De Ordinatione Fratrum. POLEMICAL WORKS, I, p. 89.

40. SELECT ENGLISH WORKS, vol. III, p. 417.
41. *De Ordinatione Fratrum*, POLEMICAL WORKS, I, p. 103.
42. POLEMICAL WORKS, I, p. 193.
43. *De Apostasia*, p. 32.
44. SELECT ENGLISH WORKS, vol. III, p. 372.
45. Ibid., p. 299.
46. Ibid., p. 299.
47. Ibid., p. 374.
48. Ibid., p. 376.
49. POLEMICAL WORKS, I, p. 97.
50. Translation by Ford Lewis Battles in Library of Christian Classics, vol. XIV, ADVOCATES OF REFORM, p. 52.
51. "C. Carmelitas, A. Augustinenses, J. Jacobitas et M. Minores significat." *Trialogus*, IV, p. 362.
52. See Chapter 5.
53. Workman, II, p. 93.
54. STUDIES IN THE HISTORY AND METHOD OF SCIENCE. THE SCIENTIFIC VIEWS AND VISIONS OF SAINT HILDEGARD, Charles Singer, p. 6.
55. SELECT ENGLISH WORKS, vol. III, p. 421.
56. THE RELIGIOUS ORDERS IN ENGLAND, vol. II, p. 92.
57. William Langland: PIERS THE PLOWMAN, Ed. W. W. Skeat, C. Passus IX. L. 79.
58. ENGLISH MONKS AND THE SUPPRESSION OF THE MONASTERIES, p. 231.
59. THE EVOLUTION OF THE MONASTIC IDEAL, H. B. Workman, p. 315.
60. *Defensio Curatorum*, p. 48.
61. Ibid., p. 72.
62. THE WORKS OF GEOFFREY CHAUCER, Ed. F. N. Robinson, p. 19.
63. Ibid., p. 20.
64. Ibid., p. 94.
65. THE NATURE AND THE EFFECT OF THE HERESY OF THE FRATICELLI, p. 137.
66. FRANCISCAN POVERTY, M. D. Lambert, p. 164.
67. *Opera Omnia*, p. 462. Quoted in STUDIES IN ENGLISH FRANCISCAN HISTORY, A. G. Little, p. 63.

68. STUDIES IN ENGLISH FRANCISCAN HISTORY, p. 68,
69. *Defensio Curatorum*, p. 40.
70. Ibid., p. 54.
71. Liber Sextus, p. 138.
72. Langland, B. Passus XX. L. 278 f.
73. Langland, C. Passus VII. L. 120 f.
74. THE WORKS OF GEOFFREY CHAUCER, Ed. F. N. Robinson, p. 18.
75. ENGLISH FRIARS AND ANTIQUITY IN THE EARLY FOURTEENTH CENTURY, Beryl Smalley, p. 42.
76. Ibid., p. 306.
77. LITERATURE AND PULPIT IN MEDIEVAL ENGLAND, G. R. Owst, p. 185.
78. THE EVOLUTION OF THE MONASTIC IDEAL, p. 288.
79. THE RELIGIOUS ORDERS IN ENGLAND, vol. II, p. 114.
80. *De Ecclesia*, p. 153.
81. SELECT ENGLISH WORKS, vol. II, p. 159.
82. Ibid., III, 217.
83. See Chapter 1, p. 23f.
84. See Chapter 5.
85. *De Ecclesia*, pp. 45–6.
86. SELECT ENGLISH WORKS, vol. III, p. 203.
87. *Opus Evangelicum*, vol. I, p. 261.
88. SELECT ENGLISH WORKS, vol. III, p. 288.
89. Ibid., p. 462.
90. Ibid., p. 112. Tract *Ave Maria*.
91. Quoted by Bernard Manning, "The Peoples' Faith in the time of Wyclif", p. 99.
92. SELECT ENGLISH WORKS, vol. III, p. 262.
93. *De Ecclesia*, p. 566.
94. SELECT ENGLISH WORKS, vol. III, p. 260.
95. Ibid., p. 259.
96. Quoted by G. G. Coulton: "Medieval Studies", No. 8, p. 8.
97. CAMBRIDGE MEDIEVAL HISTORY, vol. VII, p. 501.
98. REFORMATION WRITINGS OF MARTIN LUTHER, vol. I, B. Lee Woolf, p. 341.

CHAPTER THREE

The Remedy of an Englishman

THE FOURTEENTH CENTURY was marked by the
steady growth of nationalism in England. The country
was passing from medieval feudalism to nationhood
and like an adolescent she became aware, sometimes belliger-
ently, of her new powers and potentialities. The Hundred
Years War began in 1337 and soon assumed the character of
a national war against a national enemy with Parliament
itself responsible for the successful prosecution of hostilities.
English people began to be patriotic and the victories of
Crecy, Calais, Poitiers and, later, Agincourt stirred their
hearts. Local animosities were forgotten in the unity of the
common fight. The booty brought back from France made
the eye glisten and the impression that there were fresh
worlds for the English archers to conquer produced a
national spirit which not even the scourge of the Black
Death in 1349 nor the subsequent inefficiencies and defeats
of the protracted war could subdue.

At the same time there was the growth of English as
a national language. The antipathy against the French
mounted with the duration of the war and in 1362 a statute
was passed that all the proceedings in the law courts should
be conducted in English. Children began to learn English in
the schools. John of Trevisa, translating in 1385 the monk
Higden who was at St. Werburgh's, Chester, in the middle of
the century wrote: "In all the grammar schools of England,
children leave French and construe and learn in English. . . .
The advantage is that they learn their grammar in less time
than children used to do but the disadvantage is that now

57

grammar school children know no more French than their left heel." The poetry of Chaucer enriched and popularized the developing language within the limited circle of its readers. The influence of "The Vision of William concerning Piers the Plowman" and of the English works of John Gower were to prove considerable. Englishmen wrote and spoke as Englishmen.

There were other factors which need only be mentioned— the increasing scope of the work and powers of the Commons, so well illustrated in the "Good" Parliament of 1376, the patriotic appeal of Edward III, the gradual transfer of much jurisdiction from the Church courts, with their loyalty to Rome, to the courts of the Crown, and the growing resentment amongst all classes of the English, but especially amongst the intelligent and powerful laity, at the interference of the Pope in the ecclesiastical affairs of England and at the never-ending stream of money which flowed out to Avignon to the benefit of England's greatest enemy. On this kind of soil the seeds of nationalism grew fast.

With this nationalistic sentiment Wyclif was largely in sympathy. Admittedly he was no lover of wars, nationalistic or otherwise, and his patriotism had no jingoistic ring. Indeed in one notable passage in his English works he wrote as a pure pacifist. He refuted the popular arguments for justifying war, contended that men should not be fighters but "martirs for the love of God", and concluded, "But I read not in God's law that Christian men should excel in fighting or battle, but in meek patience. And this is the means whereby we should have God's peace".[1] With such strong convictions Wyclif was no supporter of the Hundred Years War over which the English became in turn so enthusiastic and so exasperated, but with the other movements in the direction of nationalism he allied himself. In his English sermons and tracts and in the translation of the Bible which he instigated, the English people were addressed as a nation, in their own tongue. As a literary critic says of these works, "their true significance lies in their instinctive feeling for their larger audience".[2]

Wyclif's attachment to native political institutions and his opposition to the interference of the Papacy can best be seen in his own political career. It is significant that when he went to Bruges in 1374 he did so as the emissary of the Crown to treat with the representatives of the Pope. He was no great diplomat, but the excursion made clear the direction of his sympathies and in the clash between King and Pope, between England and Rome, he was the King's man—*peculiaris regis clericus* he called himself—and an Englishman. In 1377 Parliament and the King consulted Wyclif as to "whether the realm might not legitimately stop the export of gold to Rome, considering the necessities of her defence", though Aubrey Gwynn dismisses this question as a trick opening for a political pamphlet.[3] Wyclif's answer was in *Determinacio ad argumenta Wilhelmi Vyrinham*[4] put into the mouths of seven lords. The Pope had no authority to receive tribute, so said *secundus dominus*, and it was right to break faith, argued *quintus dominus*, with one whose predecessor had made such a dishonest pact as Innocent III had made with King John. Reason, the law of Christ, the dictates of conscience and the welfare of the State combined to say that the money should be kept in England. Wyclif argued that those who had gone before endowed not the whole Church but particularly the Church of England and to send their money to the Pope would be to do injury to them *in purgatorio*.[5] The only conceivable basis on which money could be sent to the Pope was one of charity and he believed that charity began at home. Consequently, his appeal was for the nation to be trained in unanimity and endurance so that this policy could be effectively carried out. It would be no exaggeration to say that in 1377 Wyclif was the national champion against those encroachments of the Papacy to which Englishmen were objecting ever more strongly. Towards the end of this year the University of Oxford was forced to consider the Bull sent them previously containing instructions to arrest Wyclif, but he and his friends came to the agreement of a "house arrest" in order that "they should not imprison a man of the King of England at the command

59

of the Pope, lest they should seem to give the Pope lordship and regal power in England".[6]

In the dispute over the Right of Sanctuary in 1378, Wyclif again revealed himself as the defender of the rights of the English State. The position was that two knights, Haulay and Shakyl, had been committed to the Tower for refusing to produce a Spanish hostage, by name Alphonso, whom they regarded as their private and lawful prize but whom the government wanted as part exchange for a number of English imprisoned in Spain. In the summer of 1378 the two prisoners escaped from the Tower and took sanctuary in Westminster Abbey. They were followed by the authorities, who enticed Shakyl outside the precincts and arrested him and then entered the abbey and killed Haulay, together with an abbey official who came to his rescue, by the tomb of Edward the Confessor. On the particular issue of this murder the State was clearly in the wrong, though Wyclif argued in *De Ecclesia* (where his submission to Parliament has found its way into a volume of theology already quite long enough) that, in extenuation, "the man who was killed was the first to fight and to desecrate the Church".[7] His plea that the King's officers could be excused as Haulay and Shakyl were offenders against the law of God and the Church is not in the least convincing.

On the general issue of the way in which the Sanctuary right defeated the ends of justice by allowing criminals and debtors to escape almost unpunished to continue their nefarious practices the State had a case, but it was a case for changing the law and not one justifying the breaking of an existing law. The Right of Ecclesiastical Sanctuary was very ancient. It is found in the promulgations of Ine, King of Wessex in 680, and again in 857 Alfred stipulated the conditions under which Sanctuary could be granted. Ethelred (*c.* 1000) made the regulation which is found in the later Anglo-Norman laws that, though the life of a criminal in the Sanctuary must be spared, compensation of some kind must be made by the offender. After the Conquest this often took the form of abjuring the realm within forty days.

The first reference to Sanctuary in the Statutes of the Realm is in the first Statute of Edward II (1315–16) under the head of *Articuli Cleri*. There the Answer says, "They that abjure the Realm so long as they be in the Common Way, shall be in the King's Peace, nor ought to be disturbed of any Man; and when they be in the Church, their keepers ought not to abide in the Church yard, except Necessity or Peril of Escape do require so. And so long as they be in the Church, they shall not be compelled to flee away, but they shall have Necessaries for the Living and may go forth to empty their Belly".[8] In the light of this the State's case could not legitimately be a defence of the action of the King's officers but only an argument for the end of the Sanctuary Law.

This argument Wyclif also presented in *De Ecclesia*. God's law provided no refuge for debtors or criminals ("The law of Christ is an adversary to the sinner"[9]) nor did the common law (though this as we have seen was a doubtful assertion) and no privilege should be contrary to these two. The Right of Sanctuary was simply a licence to sin. If the Church insisted on so protecting the wicked, the realm itself stood in danger and that Wyclif regarded as a disaster of some magnitude. The feeble legislation which ensued in the following year did little to remedy the situation and the Sanctuary Right at Westminster, "as granted by the noble kings Edgar, St. Edward and other kings their successors",[10] was confirmed. The relevant point, however, is that the whole affair revealed Wyclif as the staunch supporter of the English State.

That Wyclif's nationalism came from genuine conviction is not, one would think, open to question. No doubt he derived a certain advantage from it. For a year or two at least it gave him popular favour and powerful protectors, but the careless way in which he tossed both aside is evidence that he was not the man to base his attitudes on the convenience of the moment. He was an Englishman not only by birth, but by conviction.

Before we examine Wyclif's proposals for reforming the

Church, which were considerably influenced by this national-istic outlook, we must give consideration to that scholastic theory of Dominion which was always in the back of his mind when he came to wrestle with the problems of Church and State. Though abstract in itself the theory had such practical consequences in Wyclif's total scheme that it must be reckoned with at this point.

De Dominio Divino, an early work of his written at Oxford, begins with the question, "What is dominion?" and the answer is that it is "A habit of the reasonable nature"[11] when set in authority over other things. The basis of the theory follows: "God rules not indirectly through the rule of subject vassals, as other kings have dominion, since immed-iately and of Himself He makes, sustains and governs all that He possesses, and helps in the accomplishment of its work according to the other uses which He requires".[12] This means that all men are the direct tenants of God and the dominion which they exercise comes straight from Him. The next step in the doctrine is to assert, as Wyclif did in the sister work *De Civili Dominio,* that "no-one who is in mortal sin has naturally a right to the gift of God".[13] He then quoted Augustine, "Sin is nothing and men when they sin become nothing",[14] and said that a man who was nothing could possess nothing. Such a person in mortal sin, lacking *caritas,* had alienated his lord-in-chief and denied him his lawful service. Therefore it was impossible for him to exercise lordship and to have that dominion which is "just in respect to God". The "possession" which he was allowed was appear-ance only, a lordship "appropriated falsely and under pretence".

Wyclif then turned to the righteous. "Every righteous man is lord over the whole sensible world".[15] He alone had a right to rule and all things belonged to him, but because no more than one man could possess all things if possession were an act of individualism, this inevitably led him to say, "all men ought to hold all things in common, so that all things ought to be communal",[16] a sentence which some of his opponents would like, without justification, to connect intimately with

62

the Peasants' Revolt. This was an idealistic communism for an idealistic world and though the precise influence it had upon John Ball and his friends is impossible to determine, it could not have been very great.

The anarchical possibilities of the theory are avoided because God permits the wicked, not dominion, but "power" over, or "use" of, property, and the righteous are therefore not free at the present time to assert their lordship over what they alone are really entitled to possess. As the Carlyles point out,[17] Wyclif means that the man in mortal sin has neither political authority nor property (and "*dominium*" is used of both), in the full and proper "evangelical" sense, but, he does not mean that he cannot have these in the ordinary or legal sense. The righteous for their part have to submit to the discipline of civil dominion, forfeiting their right to rebel, even against a tyrant, and this is the meaning of his apparently outrageous utterance that God ought to obey the devil.

The theory of Dominion has been criticized on several grounds. It has been pointed out that it is not a particularly original doctrine, Wyclif having met it in Fitzralph's *De Pauperie Salvatoris*, a copy of which reached Merton College in 1356. This in its turn, it has been argued,[18] was taken from the Augustinian theory as it is found in Giles of Rome and William of Cremona, though they would have none of Wyclif's individualism and insisted that all lordship must be exercised mediately, through the Church. Egidius Colonna and James of Viterbo have also been mentioned as possible sources, though without proof. What Wyclif did was to push the doctrine on towards its logical conclusion, a process which one critic describes as "individualism gone mad".[19]

The doctrine undoubtedly had the dead hand of the past upon it. The conceptions of "lordship" and "lord-in-chief" were typical of feudalism, and feudalism was destined to pass. Wyclif quoted the feudal common law that it was not permissible for an inferior lord to alienate property without the licence of his lord-in-chief and this was his illustration of the relationship of the wicked to God. Again, his argument in Book III of *De Dominio Divino*[20] that lordship was not

63

proprietary was based on the feudal analogy. This feudal spirit was accompanied by a devotion to scholastic methods of argument and that endless expatiation which was the delight of the schoolmen and the exasperation of their readers. *De Dominio Divino* and *De Civili Dominio* are not exceptions.

"Dominion" is a theory which never escapes from its strait-jacket of idealism and abstraction and it is apparent that Wyclif never worked it out seriously in terms of the fourteenth-century scene. Two illustrations of this will suffice. His hope, for the Church at least, was set on the abolition of civil dominion rather than its transformation. "It is plain to me that the law of the gospel is sufficient by itself without the civil law, or that called canonical, for the perfect rule of the Church militant".[21] The late medieval Church was hardly ready for this. Then there is the question, If only the righteous are allowed real lordship over property, who is to determine who are the righteous? Wyclif left this question unanswered. Presumably, since the answer is not self-evident, it could only be that the secular power must be the judge and perhaps even Wyclif shrank from making the fourteenth-century state the arbiter of private morals.

The bridge between this academic theory of Dominion and the nationalism of which we have already taken notice was Wyclif's plan for the disendowment of the Church. The link with the doctrine of Dominion was that property could not really be held by those in sin and since the Church was in sin she ought to yield up her possessions. It is quite true that in *De Civili Dominio*, after having made it clear that if the possession of temporal goods was a hindrance to the clergy in carrying out the law of Christ they must be deprived of them, he took refuge in the statement that to decide whether or not these conditions prevailed in the Church then existing "is not my province".[22] At the same time we have seen from his attacks on the Church just what his opinion of her state was. The truth is that as the years passed by he became convinced that the Church deserved to be disendowed.

Disendowment would have reduced the whole Church to

"evangelical poverty" and Wyclif did not shrink in his later thinking from drawing this drastic conclusion. He argued that when temporal possessions led the Church into the lust of lordship, into entanglement with the affairs of this life, into avarice and neglect of the preaching of the Gospel, and when they became "an occasion for contention, quarrels, or rights, to the disturbance of the Church",[23] then the only thing to do was to take them away. This was a considerable undertaking, as the wealth and possessions of the Church were immense and increasing all the time due to the universal habit of making her the only recipient of endowments and benefactions, a habit which Wyclif would gladly have changed. ("For I say it would be both useful and honourable for the Church to abrogate her many endowments".[24]) The size of the undertaking was no deterrent to Wyclif's theorizing. Disendowment must proceed at once and the Church must return to that state of poverty in which she began. The clergy must live on the free-will gifts of the people and all tithes and settled property should be renounced. "Wyclif", wrote Melanchthon somewhat scathingly, "contends that it is not lawful for priests to have any property".[25] Such severe renunciation was the only way to recapture the pristine purity of the early days. This doctrine accounts for Wyclif's affinity with the Spiritual Franciscans—"Neither Christ nor his disciples had any worldly dominion", said Mardisle, a Minorite, at the King's Council of 1374. This explains why in *De Civili Dominio* he thought of the friars as belonging to the army of "all evangelical men",[26] but whilst the Franciscans would have restricted evangelical poverty to the Mendicants, for Wyclif it was the panacea for the ills of the whole Church.

The link which disendowment had with nationalism was Wyclif's view that the only authority capable of performing the act of disendowment was the State. It was part of the theory of Dominion to keep the spiritual and temporal authorities apart. "The two swords go not into one sheath" wrote Freidank the Minnesinger in the thirteenth century, and Wyclif would have agreed with him. But this separation was on the assumption that the Church was in evangelical poverty, unencumbered with the things of this world. If she was not, and insisted on trying to serve both God and Mammon, then it was the duty of the State to step in, exert its rights and confiscate her worldly possessions. "Wherefore if God indubitably exists" (Wyclif has just argued that if He exists He is bound to provide a remedy for every evil) "then the Lords temporal are able legitimately and meritoriously to take away the wealth of an offending Church".[27] In this matter he believed wholeheartedly that the powers that be are ordained of God.

When we look at the precise way in which Wyclif proposed to effect and maintain this policy of disendowment we can see that this is the remedy of a nationalist, for the person who is given a prominent place in the scheme of things is the King. In *De Civili Dominio* he argued that in view of man's sinful nature the most desirable state of affairs was to be governed by kings according to a civil law[28] and in *De Ecclesia* he wrote affectionately of *rex noster*.[29] The exact function of the monarchy is worked out at some length in *De Officio Regis* where the rather artificial doctrine is advanced that "the king bears the image of Christ's Godhead as the priest does the image of his manhood".[30] Even bad kings bore this image and in virtue of it they must be obeyed, wrote Wyclif quoting 1 Peter 2:18: "Servants be in subjection to your masters".[31] Because of this image their regal function was to exercise superiority over the Church and the clergy in temporal matters, an assertion which had been made previously in *De Civili Dominio*.[32] This involved the act of disendowment and the employment of good lay ministers with the forfeited revenues. It was the King's responsibility to see that in his kingdom all civil possessions were in secular hands. Bearing "the image of Christ's Godhead" also meant that he must ensure that the *statum cleri* was as God intended it should be, and this involved punishing degenerate clergy, making certain that they all lived simply upon tithes and private alms and seeing that the bishops examined regularly the state of the clergy in their dioceses.

66

Wyclif was at pains to point out that the King to whom these high tasks were entrusted by God must be a man of virtue and justice and in all things set an example to his subjects. He must obey voluntarily the laws which his subjects have no choice but to obey, and be a man "to whom God has committed virtue to rule his people efficiently in conformity with his laws".[33] Wyclif also had something to say about elective kingship, but though he used the word *eleccio* and spoke about people "making their own head"[34] it is doubtful if he was advocating a full-blown republicanism, for he held up England as an example of what he wanted. Presumably he meant that in a general sense kingship must rest upon the will of the people. To sum up the fundamental position of the book, "the kingly power is obviously greater than the priestly power in temporal affairs", and "the priestly power is greater in spiritual affairs",[35] though Wyclif was more tolerant towards interference from the King than from the priest. This led inevitably to the disendowment of the Church and her return, under the King, to evangelical poverty. Whilst there is no objectionable nationalism in all this there is something of fourteenth-century patriotism, and as Wyclif worked out the intricacies of his arguments and answered all the possible objections in *De Officio Regis* the thought was always present that the English have *unum regem benedictum*.

It is not difficult to criticize Wyclif's policy of disendowment. The King might well be totally unfitted to perform the considerable tasks which the scheme imposed upon him. Though he met this objection in the abstract (the power of bad rulers was still committed to them by God) he did not face what this would mean in practice. When one remembers the life of Edward II, his preference for bad advice over good, his oppression of the Church, his neglect of justice and his preoccupation with trivialities, one can see that Wyclif's scheme was hardly likely to be a resounding success. When one recalls the way in which both Edward III and Richard II worked hand in glove with the Papacy to defeat the intention of the Statute of Provisors and secure lucrative benefits for their servants and friends (surely the worst example was Robert Stretten who was rejected even by Avignon *propter defectum literaturae* but was prised into the bishopric of Coventry and Lichfield by the Black Prince and his father) and all their other intrigues with the Popes, one has no great faith in their capacity to reform the Church. The characters of these men—Edward III with his self-indulgence and wild temper and Richard II with his despotic self-will—inspire no confidence whatever in Wyclif's scheme.

When the nobility were associated with the King in the implementation of this policy, as they were in the later, English works of Wyclif, the undesirability of his suggestions becomes even more obvious. How could men like John of Gaunt be entrusted with the reform of the Church? And with so much wealth at stake the prospect of what would happen during the reign of an infant is alarming. The seizure of all ecclesiastical treasure by the King and its disbursement to his friends, in the process of which, as one scholar says, "the poor would undoubtedly have come off rather empty-handed and the rich would only have become richer",[36] would have produced a last state worse than the first.

Bearing in mind the extent of all Wyclif's criticisms of the medieval Church—criticisms which may well have been contributions to Reform in their own right—the remedy of disendowment seems to founder on the rock of impracticable idealism. Did Wyclif really believe that the evils of the Papacy, the Caesarean clergy, the monks, the friars, the medieval practices on which he expatiated at such length would be solved by handing over temporal possessions and reforming authority to the King and his baronial friends and rehabilitating the Church in the simple, unpretentious garb of the first century without reference to all that had happened since? Presumably he did, as he suggests no other programme for reform. But immediately one turns from the ideal to the possible one sees that the Church would simply have become the lackey, and the unreformed lackey, of a not over-scrupulous oligarchy. It has been suggested in defence of the scheme that Wyclif campaigned for complete disendowment in the hope of obtaining a partial confiscation of wealth after the fashion of a modern wage-claim, but this does less than justice to the relentless logic of his mind which insisted on pushing his theories to their conclusion regardless of whether they were practical or not, and in this case quite obviously they were not. That the issue was temporarily shelved by the events of the Peasants' Revolt was no bad thing.

At the same time the unworkability of Wyclif's scheme in the fourteenth century should not obscure the fact that his disendowment policy was a real contribution to Reform. He caught up the spirit of men like Arnold of Brescia and Joachim of Fiore and passed on this restive and reforming urge until in one form or another it found its expression in the Church-State relationships formulated at the time of the Reformation. There may be no linear development between the Dissolution of the Monasteries or the Lutheran Doctrine of the State[37] and John Wyclif's scholastic tracts on disendowment, but that the latter by its very existence helped to prepare the way for the former is undeniable.

The same is true of the office of the King and the importance of the secular arm. History followed the path adumbrated by Wyclif, and Henry VIII could not have wanted more authority than Wyclif was willing to give him in De Officio Regis. As J. T. McNeill says, Henry VIII gave the English Church "a moderate dose of Wyclif's medicine",[38] and the Acts of Supremacy would have made pleasant reading for Wyclif. In recognizing the King as the lawful head of the State and of the Church, in temporal concerns at least, Wyclif sounded a note not displeasing to the English ear and one which would be heard again and again when Reform came into its own. As Matthew Spinka puts it, "the measures advocated by Wyclif in De Officio Regis—the principle of a territorial Church governed by the king—were actually realized in the days of Henry VIII and his successors (except Mary)".[39] Some scholars go even further, and R. W. and A. J. Carlyle, after a succinct summary of Wyclif's political theory, argue that his point of departure from the

Middle Ages is the "conception of the duty of absolute obedience to the prince",[40] an idea not far removed from the Divine Right of Kings (described by Kern as "a legal claim on the part of a king to unconditional obedience"[41]).

As far as the doctrine of Dominion itself is concerned it is marked by an attention to individualism which we shall notice again in Wyclif's theology and which here as there looks forward to the Reformation. As Shirley pointed out in his introduction to *Fasciculi Zizaniorum*, the doctrine was, from a scholastic point of view, to do the work later done much more adequately by the doctrine of Justification by Faith. "The emancipation of the individual conscience was the aim of both".[42] All men being the direct tenants of God foreshadowed all men being saved by their own personal faith. G. G. Coulton supports this. "The real kernel of the Reformation, doctrinally," he writes, "was a conviction of the soul's direct responsibility to God"[43] and this is the link he finds between Luther's doctrine of Justification by Faith and Wyclif's theory of Dominion.

Again, the nationalism which we have noticed in Wyclif's politics, in his opposition to the Right of Sanctuary and in the disendowment theory which followed upon his doctrine of Dominion, was forward-looking. The Reformation saw the final breaking up of the unity of medieval Christendom into the separate nation-states of the modern world, and in the process which led up to that historic transition due importance must be given to the thought of Wyclif. The loyalties of men turned from the great Mother-Church of the West centred (Avignon apart) in Rome to the institutions, sacred and secular, of their own lands; and the thoughts and theories of John Wyclif gave encouragement to that process. It would be an exaggeration to say that he had any full realization of the end in view once he escaped from the realm of pure theory. In practical affairs he was much more the whole-hearted protestant against current evils than the architect of things to come, but it so happened that he was on the side of history. The future proved to be with nationalism and the remedy of Wyclif for the sickness of the medieval Church was, for all its academic remoteness, the remedy of an Englishman for the English.

REFERENCES

1. SELECT ENGLISH WORKS, vol. III, p. 138.
2. J. P. Whitney, p. 66, ch. II, vol. II, CAMBRIDGE HISTORY OF ENGLISH LITERATURE.
3. THE ENGLISH AUSTIN FRIARS IN THE TIME OF WYCLIF, Aubrey Gwynn, p. 250.
4. *Opera Minora*, p. 415.
5. *Fasciculi Zizaniorum*, p. 262.
6. *Eulogium Historiarum*, vol. III. *Continuatio Eulogii*. RS. Trans. Trevelyan, ENGLAND IN THE AGE OF WYCLIF, p. 84.
7. *De Ecclesia*, p. 150.
8. Quoted J. C. Cox, THE SANCTUARIES AND SANCTUARY SEEKERS OF MEDIEVAL ENGLAND, p. 18.
9. *De Ecclesia*, p. 226.
10. J. C. Cox, p. 53.
11. *De Dominio Divino*, p. 2.
12. Ibid., p. 33.
13. *De Civili Dominio*, I, p. 1.
14. Ibid., p. 3.
15. Ibid., p. 47.
16. Ibid., p. 96.
17. A HISTORY OF MEDIEVAL POLITICAL THEORY IN THE WEST, vol. VI, R. W. and A. J. Carlyle, p. 57.
18. THE ENGLISH AUSTIN FRIARS IN THE TIME OF WYCLIF, p. 59 f.
19. THE SOCIAL AND POLITICAL IDEAS OF SOME GREAT MEDIEVAL THINKERS, F. J. C. Hearnshaw, p. 213.
20. *De Dominio Divino*, p. 201 f.
21. *De Civili Dominio*, I, p. 121.
22. Ibid., p. 269.
23. Ibid., p. 268.
24. *De Simonia*, p. 37.

25. Preface to *Sententiae veterum de Coena Domini* in a letter to Myconius, *c.* 1530.
26. *De Civili Dominio*, I, p. 328.
27. Ibid., p. 267.
28. Ibid., p. 185.
29. *De Ecclesia*, p. 338.
30. *De Officio Regis*, p. 13.
31. Ibid., p. 5.
32. *De Civili Dominio*, I, p. 270.
33. *De Officio Regis*, p. 142.
34. Ibid., p. 249.
35. Ibid., pp. 142-3.
36. THE ORIGINS OF THE REFORMATION, James Mackinnon, p. 86.
37. Though just how Erastian this was is a matter for debate. See THE THEOLOGY OF MARTIN LUTHER, H. H. Kramm, ch. VII. Gordon Rupp says (THE RIGHTEOUSNESS OF GOD, p. 287): "No teaching of Luther has been more misrepresented than his teaching about the nature, extent and limits of temporal power".
38. JOURNAL OF RELIGION, VII, p. 466 (1927).
39. ADVOCATES OF REFORM. Library of Christian Classics, vol. XIV, p. 25.
40. A HISTORY OF MEDIEVAL POLITICAL THEORY IN THE WEST, vol. VI, p. 62.
41. KINGSHIP AND LAW IN THE MIDDLE AGES, F. Kern, p. 138.
42. *Fasciculi Zizaniorum*, p. lxvi.
43. MEDIEVAL PANORAMA, G. G. Coulton, p. 490.

CHAPTER FOUR

Wyclif and the Bible

WYCLIF WAS CALLED *Doctor Evangelicus* because of his love for the Bible and his constant reference to it, and Christian thought since the Reformation has always linked his name with the sacred book. Two questions are involved in his relationship to the Bible. They can be treated separately, though in the work of Wyclif they are inextricably joined. One is the famous translations associated with his name and the other is the appeal to the authority of Scripture to replace the (to him) discredited authority of the medieval Church. In both he made a positive and significant contribution to Reform.

It would not be true to claim that the translations inspired by Wyclif were the first translations into English of Holy Scripture. Sir Thomas More, whose interest lay in the permission or refusal of the Church to read translations as much as in the translations themselves, made this not unbiased statement: "For ye shal understande that the great arche heretike Wickliffe, whereas the hole byble was long before his dayes by vertuous and wel lerned men translated into the English tong, and by good and godly people with deucion and sobrenes wel and reverently red, toke upon hym of a malicious purpose to translate it of new".[1] But More's knowledge was not accurate and it must not be assumed from what he said that English translations were common and popular before Wyclif's time. John Lewis wrote in 1719, "It is a mistake of Sir Thomas More, and some others since his time, to affirm, that before Dr. Wiclif's time there were old translations of the Bible into the English spoken after the conquest".[2]

The truth is that there were translations of parts of the Bible in existence—Bede had translated part of the Fourth Gospel ("And Sistrence in his fifte booke . . . seith the euangelie of John was drawen into Englice be the for seide Bede"[3]), there were some few Anglo-Saxon Gospels and Richard Rolle had translated the Psalter as King Alfred before him was supposed to have done . . . but that these were in any sense generally known or widely read cannot be substantiated. Bede's translation would be mostly used inside the monasteries (though Beryl Smalley produces evidence[4] that St. Boniface found his works on the lessons for the year and the Proverbs of Solomon a help in his missionary work) and the earliest Anglo-Saxon Gospels were glosses which were of use for private study, but not for general reading. Rolle's translation too was designed to help the religious in their monasteries and not the laity in their parishes and it included glosses as well as the text. There existed also paraphrases of the text and rhyming verses based upon it which cannot be classed as strict translations though they were of more use pastorally. As Margaret Deanesly points out,[5] if orthodox translations had existed on any scale, particularly in the period immediately before Wyclif, the opposition to the translations associated with him would be inexplicable. The evidence all points to the fact that there was no widespread reading of the Scriptures in the vernacular and that when Wyclif deliberately took the step of instigating a translation he was breaking with the general tradition.

If it is conceded that Bible-reading is a necessary part of Christian practice and essential for a healthy Church then there could be no argument about the need in the fourteenth century. When the qualifications for institution to a benefice were the ability to recite a few Latin formulae by heart and to read and sing the Mass in Latin, and when the ordinary Christian in England knew no more of "Goddis lawe" than some jingle he had picked up from a passing friar or some garbled illustration from a sermon, one can understand the concern of Wyclif who believed that "every Christian ought to study this book because it is the whole truth".[6] He main-

74

tained that since the time of the Decretals the honour paid and the importance given to the Bible had steadily declined, and G. G. Coulton supports this view when he points out[7] that in most surviving medieval Bibles it is hard to find any trace of wear, even where we might most confidently expect it, e.g. in the Psalms or the Gospels. Knowledge of a kind could be obtained from the Sunday Homilies, the pictures on church walls and in church windows or from the rough-and-ready miracle plays, and when that was not enough the fourteenth-century Christian had to find what solace he could in the couplet:

> Though ye understand it nought
> Ye may well wit that God it wrought.

Wyclif saw in this state of affairs the need to place in his hands a Bible which he could read. "Christ and his apostles taught the people in that tongue that was best known to them. Why should men not do so now?"[8] If it could be done, as it had been in German and in French, why not in English?

The actual translations made under the inspiration of Wyclif have come down to us in two versions. The first is a literal, word-for-word translation, after the fashion of Rolle, of the Vulgate, the fourteenth-century text of which was, as Westcott points out,[9] "far from pure". Its literalism sometimes led to meaninglessness. *"Quid nobis et tibi, Jesu fili dei"* we find, for example, translated "What to us, and to thee, Jesus the Son of God".[10] The most notable example of confusion is from 1 Samuel 2: 10[11] where the Latin *Dominum formidabunt adversarii ejus* is translated in the first version as "The Lord shulen drede the aduersaries of him" and in the second version "Aduersaries of the Lord schulen drede him", the literal translation reversing the meaning of the Vulgate. The scribe's desire to keep the words in their original order was stronger at this point than his regard for the rules of grammar. Even where no confusion results, the method of literal translation does not lead to a smooth prose. In St. Matthew 13: 11, where the Latin is *Qui respondens ait*, this version has the literal, "The which answerynge seith"

75

which the later version amends to "And he answeride and seide". The original manuscript of the first version from the beginning of Genesis to Baruch 3: 20 is extant and bears the marks of five different hands. A contemporary copy breaking off at Baruch 3: 20 adds the words, *"explicit translationem Nicholay de Herford"* and then continues with the Old Testament and most of the New. Nicholas of Hereford left the country in 1382, so presumably the group of Wycliffite scholars with whom he had been working, of whom Purvey, Wyclif's "secretary", must have been one, concluded the work in his absence.

The second version, also from the Vulgate and therefore closely related to the first, is, as we have noticed, more idiomatic, or "openlier" as the General Prologue has it, and can be dated about 1396. An example of its freer translation can be seen in Genesis 3: 8. The Latin is *"abscondit se Adam et uxor eius a facie Domini Dei"*. The first version renders this literally, "Adam hid hym and his wijf fro the face of the Lord God", but the second version has the more idiomatic, "Adam and his wijf hidden hem fro the face of the Lord God".[12] The author of the Prologue lists the rules he followed to make the second version more idiomatic. The ablative absolute, for example, may be resolved into the verb with a particle prefixed such as *the while, for, if, when, after* or *and*. The illustration given in the Prologue itself is:[13]

Latin	*Arescentibus hominibus prae timore*
Version 1	Men waxinge drye for drede
Version 2	For men schulen wexe drye for drede.

There is a further example in Genesis 13: 10:[14]

Latin	*Elevatis itaque Loth oculis vidit omnem circa regionem Iordanis*
Version 1	And so Loth, his eyen heud up, sawe al the regioun abowt of Jordan.
Version 2	And so Loth reiside his izen, and seiz aboute al the cuntrei of Jordan.

Presumably it was thought that the earlier literal version was unsuitable for the general reading envisaged by Wyclif's hope, "therefore men will acknowledge Holy Writ and the living of Christ for their rule",[15] though McFarlane says this is "to pile guesswork upon ignorance".[16] It seems most likely that the author of the second version was John Purvey, for he was the only Lollard scholar sufficiently accomplished who had not recanted by 1396. The Prologue describes him as translating it with "myche travile, with diverse felawis and helperis", and to accommodate the latter Pollard would have it called the "Oxford Bible".[17]

That Wyclif himself took no major share in the academic work of translation, and apart from anything else his prolific Latin and English works could not possibly have left him time, is no denial of the fact that he was the inspiration behind the venture. From the first his name is associated with it. Knighton for example, writing before 1400, speaks scathingly of "this Master John Wyclif who translated from Latin *in Anglicam linguam non angelicam*"[18] and laments that the Bible is being vulgarized and "laid open to laity, and even to women". Hus claimed that Wyclif translated *"tota Biblia"* and Archbishop Arundel, writing to Pope John XXII at the beginning of the fifteenth century, after his uncomplimentary "pestilential and most miserable John Wyclif of damned memory" went on to say that he was responsible for a new translation "in the mother tongue". Attempts have been made to refute the conclusions to which this early testimony leads,[19] but they have not been convincing. Admittedly nothing is more difficult at this distance of time than to apportion work done to the writer and thinker himself and to the school which gathered round him. Exaggerated statements like "In Wiclif we have the acknowledged father of English prose, the first translator of the whole Bible into the language of the English people"[20] must be set aside in favour of a more cautious approach. This leads us to reject both the notion of Wyclif as the sole and omnicompetent translator and the assertion of Cardinal Gasquet that he had nothing to do with it at all and to agree with J. P. Whitney when, in commenting on the work still to be done on the Bible translations of the time, he concluded that "the name of

Wyclif will probably still be left in its old connection even if his individual share be uncertain or lessened".[21]

It should be noticed in passing that in neither of the two versions is there any attempt to insert a particular translation for doctrinal reasons, though naturally enough the prefaces and notes are not without bias. Even Dr. Gasquet admits this. "So far as I have been able to discover from an examination of the two texts, there is nothing inconsistent with their having been the work of perfectly orthodox sons of holy Church".[22] The Oxford men who did this work, and this is in the main true of all the Lollard translators, were scholars of integrity and their only motive was to provide a translation both accurate and understandable. With the second version they succeeded.

The honesty and faithfulness of the translation together with the intelligibility of the second version account for the extent of its use. Obviously the illiterate were excluded, apart from what they could learn by heart from the lips of others, and so were the very poor, for the price of a copy of the Gospels was four marks and forty pence. But those who could both afford a copy of the Wyclif Bible and then read what they had bought were not officially discouraged by the Church on the grounds that the translation was heretical. The Lollard knights would be included in this number, as Wyclif was most anxious that they should, and so would the pious priest who knew little Latin and less Greek, but by no means all the "lewid men" that Wyclif would have wished. There was some opposition to the translations because of the innate conservatism of men like the "great Bishop of England who is evil pleased that God's law is written in English",[23] and from theological oddities like Pecock who objected to translation on the strange ground that "thou shalt not find expressly in Holy Scripture that the New Testament should be written in the English tongue to laymen".[24] There was a certain amount of suspicion of the translations because of their association with the Lollard heretics, and this was amply justified by the prologues and commentaries which they added, but if the translations themselves had contained any hint of heresy the opposition would have caused every copy in the land to be burned. As it was the Church attempted to control the indiscriminate reading and translating of the Bible by insisting on the necessity for episcopal approval.

The Wycliffite translations, and particularly the first one, were undertaken because of the position which the Bible held in the thinking of Wyclif himself. He did not begin by seeing the people's need of an English Bible, indeed he says surprisingly little on the subject. Rather, his theories drove him into the position where it became a necessity to have a Bible open at first to the less learned clergy and the educated laymen (hence the word-for-word translation) and then open to all literates. The theory of Dominion, as we have seen, taught that every man was the tenant-in-chief of God and no intermediary came between them. This led to the necessity of a personal relationship between God and the Christian and an individual responsibility on the part of the tenant-in-chief to know the law of God and to keep it. It was the Bible which made this possible and Wyclif drew his own conclusion: "And so it is a help here to Christian men to study the gospel in that tongue in which they know best Christ's words".[25] This was not without its political significance, for as Margaret Deanesly points out,[26] such a translation would be a weapon in the hands of the lay party in their struggle against the clergy. Again, Wyclif's theory that the Church could be reformed only by a return to the primitive poverty of New Testament times demanded a knowledge of the Bible in which those times were described. Christians could not be expected to follow Christ in His poverty and meekness unless they could be fully informed about them first.

In addition to these particular theories it must be noticed that Wyclif appealed to the Bible at every turn as his final authority. It was, as he wrote in the opening paragraph of *De Veritate Sacrae Scripturae*, "the basis of every catholic opinion". The Bible was Christ's book. He was the beginning and the end of Scripture and faith in Him was the prerequisite of understanding it rightly. The truth of the Bible was everlasting because it reflected the Eternal Light, and its authority was complete and final. He used the expressions *verbum dei* and *verbum domini* to describe it.

Gustaf Aulén, comparing the medieval conception of the Word with the Reformed, says of the former, "The Word was significant only as doctrine and law".[27] There is unquestionably a great deal of this in Wyclif. Typical of his assertions are, "all law, all philosophy, all logic and all ethics are in Holy Scripture";[28] "a sacred Scripture which is the catholic faith";[29] the Bible is indeed "one perfect word, proceeding from the mouth of God",[30] but this is in respect of it as a source of doctrine and law. Again, he argues at length in favour of its divine origin, its sufficiency and its clarity, but only that men may be encouraged to accept it as "Goddis lawe".

A search through *De Veritate Sacrae Scripturae* for something more deeply theological is not entirely unrewarded. The Bible mediates Christ and the sentence "to ignore the Scriptures is to ignore Christ"[31] is repeated several times. Christ as the foundation of all salvation and sole redeemer of man is the subject of the Bible in all its parts.[32] Again, our response to Christ has its roots in the Holy Book, for "faith depends on the Scriptures".[33] The Holy Ghost is active in conjunction with the Bible—when Augustine wrote his commentaries "he was inspired by the Holy Spirit"[34]—but this is mostly a matter of understanding its content. The moral influence of the Scriptures is referred to[35] and there must be an ethical aim in all proclamation of its truth.[36] The Bible is the Word of God in the sense that in it God speaks through His saints[37] and it is His voice behind the printed word.[38] Because of this *scriptura sacra signat celeste misterium,* the mystery of our salvation. Most of this is an advance on the Bible regarded simply as a source of law and doctrine, but it is still short of what the Reformers meant when they spoke of the Word of God.

Wyclif's view of the all-sufficiency of Scripture sharply

distinguished him from the medieval schoolmen who recognized little if any difference between Scripture and tradition, both of which were for them part of *auctoritas*. This Wyclif would not have and he was at pains to separate his purely Biblical theology from the medieval view. Though appealing often enough to the Fathers and Doctors of the Church he put the Bible on a higher pedestal than them all, particularly in his later years.

It is made clear by Tavard[39] that the distinction between Scripture and tradition is a later and, in his judgment, unfortunate fourteenth-century development from the earlier medieval and patristic position that the two coin here. Wyclif might conceivably have been prepared to accept his statement[40] that "Scripture cannot be the Catholic faith when it is cut off from the Catholic Church. Neither can be subservient to the other", though not, one would think, the assumption that this Church was the visible, Roman one.

A case has been made out by Dom de Vooght[41] that Wyclif did not set Scripture against tradition at all, as Netter first asserted, but it has been effectively refuted by Fr. Hurley[42] who points out the development in Wyclif from medieval orthodoxy to the position defined by Knowles[43] as that "in which Scripture (as interpreted by Wyclif) is the only norm".

This position was a revolutionary one, for it meant that "Goddis lawe" must take preference over the decrees and pronouncements of Mother Church as the competent and proper authority for Christian truth and practice. From this Wyclif did not shrink. Scripture was to him the *magistrum optimum*, higher than reason or Church tradition, and doctrines were to be upheld only if they agreed with Holy Scripture. He took the theory, set out by Guido Terreni, that "the whole authority of Scripture depends upon the Church" and turned it the other way round. Such a conception led naturally to the necessity of a translation, first for those who would be aware of the issues involved in this departure and then for believers generally.

Wyclif clearly thought that such a change of authority was a practical possibility and he insisted that the meaning of

Scripture was plain even to the simple. Assiduous study on the principle of one part of the Bible interpreting the other was an asset wherever possible, but the foremost requirements were spiritual. "So the learner of Scripture does not acquire the wealth of wisdom unless with contrition he becomes humble".[44] A good life was the best guide to an adequate knowledge of holy writ. The most powerful ally to acceptance of the Bible as the supreme authority and to its understanding was preaching, and to this Wyclif gave considerable importance. "The preaching of the Word of God is an act more solemn than the making of the Sacrament".[45] "The most high service that men have in earth is to preach God's word",[46] for "Jesus Christ occupied him most in the work of preaching and last, other works".[47] "Praying is good", he said, "but not so good as preaching".[48] In *De Officio Pastorali* he urged, "Eloquence of preaching is especially necessary in curates. Among all the duties of the pastor after justice of life, holy preaching is most to be praised".[49] Its motives must always be, "for thank of God and love of saving Christian souls".[50]

His own *Sermones* contain similar comments about preaching. Christ set the example in it and to follow Him in this regard a man must give all his strength.[51] To prohibit preaching is to prevent the influence of the Spirit.[52] Taking the disciples' preaching mission as his example, he stipulated five rules for preachers.[53] They should heal sick men, including those with "goostli sekenesse"; they should raise up the dead, i.e. those dead in their sins; they should heal the leprous men, heresy being the fourteenth-century equivalent of leprosy; they should cast out fiends, which meant casting out sin; they should travel without money and beware of the temptation to simony. This preaching should, of course, be grounded in the Bible, and bishops and priests should be diligent students of Scripture. "This office" wrote Wyclif of the priesthood, "is in no way able to be performed without a knowledge of Holy Scripture",[54] and he advocated that a sermon on the Sunday gospel should be preached in every parish. In this way he hoped that men would learn to go to the holy book for their authority instead of the hierarchy of the medieval Church.

It is not surprising that in this situation Wyclif should be a fierce contender for what is now called "fundamentalism". Here he differed from the schoolmen, on whom he poured so much scorn, who sought a meaning in Scripture other than the literal one. As John Cunningham the Carmelite, who opposed Wyclif on this as on other matters, said, Scripture is true either *"ad sensum literalem"* or *"ad sensum mysticum"*,[55] and once a medieval scholar started to build up a *distinctio*[56] there was no knowing where he might stop. Wyclif did not agree with Cunningham, for he was a literalist, though he did concede in *De Officio Pastorali* in a reference to the desirability of an English translation, "that there may be faults in unfaithful translating as there might have been many faults in turning from Hebrew into Greek and from Greek into Latin".[57] But unquestionably he believed, as the schoolmen themselves were required to do officially, that Holy Scripture was an external, infallible authority. "It is impossible for any part of Holy Scripture to be wrong".[58] "In Holy Scripture is all the truth".[59]

This theory was and still is open to the double objection that the authority is not truly external, as in the last resort it is the object of a subjective choice, and that the various interpretations placed by individual consciences upon the words of Holy Scripture can be used, as they were by both schoolmen and Lollards, to support very different theological, ecclesiastical, and social systems. To this second and more practical objection Wyclif would have replied firstly that the fault lay in the reader's intelligence, and secondly that the Holy Ghost could be relied upon to teach Christians the true interpretation. Here we must notice that Wyclif's views on the interpretation of Scripture underwent a change. For some time he held, in common with other scholastics, that the best guidance could be given by reason and by the doctors of the Church, but later he looked to the Holy Ghost. "The Holy Ghost teaches us the meaning of Scripture, as Christ opened the Scriptures to the apostles".[60] In case this gave

rise to some exaggerated subjective claims Wyclif asserted
that in practice it meant that Scripture must be interpreted
by Scripture. "One part of Scripture explains another"
he wrote in *De Veritate Sacrae Scripturae*[61] and every text
must be understood in the light of the whole truth of the
Bible.

Neither, to continue with criticism, is it wise to separate
the infallible Scriptures from the tradition of the Church as
sharply as Wyclif did in his references to the *mixtim theologi*,
the "motley divines" who laid stress on both. The canon
of Scripture itself was a product of the tradition of the
Church, as Luther's opponents were not slow to point out in
the sixteenth century. Again it must be remembered that it
is dangerous to minimize tradition when "Goddis lawe"
cannot hope to deal with every eventuality of conduct. As
Bishop Pecock said, "For how shall we dare to wear breeches
which the Bible does not mention; how justify the use of
clocks to know the hour?"[62]

Such criticisms, though thoroughly justified, do not
demand an alteration of the judgment that Wyclif's attitude
to the Bible, for all it verges on bibliolatry, was one of his
most positive contributions to Reform. A hundred and fifty
years before the Reformation he pointed the way to the
only authority to which Christians could turn when they
reacted so strongly from the corruptions of the medieval
Church. As a great German student of Wyclif wrote, "He
distinctly recognized the fundamental principle of the
Reformation that the Bible is the only authority for the life
and faith of every Christian; and he put it forth with perfect
clearness and unmistakable force".[63]

The fact that Martin Luther never read *De Veritate
Sacrae Scripturae* does not mean that there is no connection
between the two. The latter prepared the way by expounding
many of the same ideas which the former obtained from other
sources and used with such effectiveness. Luther, like Wyclif,
looked beyond traditional theology to the Scriptures, though
with the advantage of being able to read them in the original,
sacred tongues. He too placed the highest value on Holy

Scripture: "Let it alone remain the judge and mistress of all books".[64] When Luther made his famous declaration before the Emperor and Diet of Worms in 1521 he did so *convictus testimoniis Scripturae*. The Bible contained everything necessary to salvation and *sola scriptura*, though not an inflexible regulation, is a principle taken very seriously by Luther, as by Wyclif. Both men also wanted a restoration of primitive, Biblical Christianity (though not in precisely the same way) which was impossible without a constant appeal to the sacred book. Luther, like Wyclif, wanted Scripture to speak for itself and his wish was "that there were no commentators and that pure Scripture as taught by the living voice should everywhere reign".[65] And where this was difficult Luther, like Wyclif, would have the "dark" words explained by the "clear" words, the Law of the Old Testament interpreted by the Gospel of the New. For both the Bible was the "cradle of Christ" and Luther measured the value of books by the extent to which they treated of Christ. "Also it is the right touchstone to judge all books when it is seen whether they study Christ or not".[66] As Philip Watson says,[67] Luther "is invariably thinking of Scripture as a witness to Christ, a vehicle of the Word". "He evaluated the worth of the various books in the Bible" says Swihart,[68] "by the degree they revealed Christ". The presence of Christ in the Bible was an assurance of its divine origin and to both Wyclif and Luther it was *verbum Dei*.

This meant more and had a wider context with Luther than it did with Wyclif. As Heinrich Bornkamm says,[69] "When we attempt to understand any part of Luther's theology it is always advisable to proceed from its very core, his view of the Word of God". "The whole life and nature of the Church exists in the Word of God".[70] Nothing is less subject to man's judgment than the Word of God. On the contrary, man is under "the government of the Word" and Luther speaks of his conscience as being "prisoner to God's Word". "All that is in scripture is through the Word brought forth into the clearest light and proclaimed to the whole world".[71] "To possess the Word of God is to possess

God, the creator of all things".[72] These were positions for the most part only adumbrated in Wyclif.

In other ways the two men were not identical in their views. Luther was not apparently the literalist and fundamentalist that Wyclif was (although according to Lutheran scholars there is some ambiguity about their subject's exact position) and one cannot think of the schoolman saying, "Some day I will use James to heat my stove".[73] Luther too saw much more clearly than Wyclif the essential difference between the Old and New Testaments, but beyond these differences the Englishman and the German were united in their insistence that the Bible was God's book and "containeth all things necessary to salvation".[74]

A similar comparison might be made with Calvin, who was, according to Mackinnon, "pre-eminently the Biblical theologian of the Reformation".[75] He was prepared to accept the Scriptures as the infallible voice of God *a spiritu sancto dictatum*:[76] "Hence the Scriptures obtain full authority among believers, only when men regard them as having sprung from heaven, as if there the living words of God were heard",[77] but he recognized that revelation in the Bible was progressive. As Wilhelm Niesel says, "He did not understand inspiration in any mechanical fashion. . . . In the Scriptural exegesis of Calvin there is nothing to suggest a belief in literal inerrancy".[78] For Calvin the Scriptures were the only authoritative witness to Christ. "Christ", he wrote, "cannot be properly known in any other way than from the Scriptures".[79] "The aim of all our attention to the Bible should be the recognition of Jesus Christ".[80] He accepted the sufficiency of the Bible and to imagine that it needed supplementing by Church tradition was "to do grievous harm to the Holy Spirit".[81] "Holy Scripture is the sole criterion of the teachings of the Church".[82] Like Wyclif, Calvin believed that the Bible could be understood through the guidance of the Holy Spirit. "We must be given eyes and ears to register the truth of the Bible if we are really to recognize and grasp it. When we turn to God, God effects this change in us through His Spirit".[83] As H. Jackson Forstman says,[84] "The Word must be taught and interpreted. For this the Spirit is necessary, but then the Spirit is tested by the Word". Under the Spirit the Bible becomes the word of life to the believer. "When by the power of the Spirit it effectually penetrates our hearts, when it conveys Christ to us, then it becomes a word of life converting the soul".[85]

To reform the Church a sufficient authority had to be found to replace the all-embracing authority of the medieval Church. It had to be absolute and unquestioned, having its source in itself and not in the Church which had determined its precise form. It was John Wyclif who persuaded those who were willing to hear that the Bible was such an authority, and this conviction of his came to be accepted by the leaders of the Reformation in the sixteenth century.

Wyclif's further contribution was made by the translations into the vernacular to which his theories drove him. His developing conviction that a sacred book could not replace a sacred institution as the source of religious authority unless that book could be read by all was one shared by the Reformers. The work of translation done under his guidance stimulated interest in the whole matter. The lawfulness of an English Bible became a serious subject for debate and under the preaching of the Lollards men came to realize that the Bible was theirs to read. Hard upon this came the invention of printing, and vernacular Bibles began to appear in increasing numbers upon the Continent. In England the change was slower, for the decrees of the Synod of Oxford in 1408 had given the impression that the reading of English Bibles was forbidden by the Church, an impression which was strengthened by their association with Lollard heresy; but with the arrival of the sixteenth century Sir Thomas More, a pillar of orthodoxy, headed the sixteenth chapter of his Dialogue, "And the author sheweth his mind, that it wer convenient to have the byble in englishe".

Erasmus played his scholarly part in the process of emancipation and reiterated the view which Wyclif had expressed a hundred years before: "I would desire that all women should read the gospel and Paul's epistles, and I would to

God they were translated into the tongues of all men, so that they might not only be known of Scots and Irishmen, but also of the Turks and Saracens".[86] Tyndale was burned at the stake for his part in making this a reality, but by this time the open Bible, so essential for the Reformation, had arrived and in 1538 Thomas Cromwell sent to Archbishop Cranmer the Royal Injunctions which commanded that a copy of Coverdale's Great Bible should be placed in every parish church for parishioners to read. On the Continent Luther followed in the steps of Wyclif as a translator and "the Bible, that is, the whole of Holy Scripture in German" appeared in 1534. The motive behind it was the same—that the common people might have immediate access to the authority behind the Faith. "It ought", said Luther, "to remain in the hands of all pious people day and night". In this long struggle Wyclif has an honoured place.

The final point must be made that the emphasis on preaching, which with Wyclif was complementary to his attitude to the Bible, was a precursor of the Reformation. The controversy over pulpit and altar was renewed in the sixteenth century. Luther demanded to know why the Romanists had not made a sacrament of preaching and lamented that "the whole world is full of priests, bishops, cardinals and clergy, not one of whom, as far as his official responsibilities go, is a preacher".[87] He believed that Christ should and must be preached in such a way that faith grows out of, and is received from, the preaching. And his comment when he noticed young people beginning a life of Roman observances was, "None of it need have happened if only the right preachers had been there".[88]

There is a similar emphasis on preaching in Calvin. "The Word goeth out of the mouth of God in such a manner that it likewise goeth out of the mouth of men; for God does not speak openly from heaven but employs men as his instruments".[89] "God does not wish to be heard but by the voice of his ministers".[90] "Here then is the sovereign power with which the pastors of the church, by whatever name they be called, ought to be endowed. That is, that they may dare boldly to do all things by God's Word".[91] Through the preaching of the Word Christ gives His sacramental presence to His Church and accomplishes His work in men's hearts and throughout the entire creation. So with Zwingli. Through his preaching ministry in Zürich, described by one historian as "electrifying",[92] he damned the political and moral evils around him and summoned men to repentance and to a scriptural faith in Christ. "Every time Zwingli mounted the pulpit steps, he realized that it was a matter of dealing seriously with the most serious of all subjects. That was his office and his holy passion".[93]

Again Wyclif is shown to be on the side of Reform. His position, that to declare the Word of God from the Bible was of more importance than "to make God's body", was where the Reformers stood. It is idle to speculate on the subsequent course of history if Wyclif had not lived and the effect this would have had upon the Reformation. One can only accept the facts as they are—that the Bible which was central to that Reformation was proclaimed as the supreme authority for the Faith and its translation into the vernacular inspired by the parish priest of Lutterworth.

REFERENCES

1. Dialogue, WORKS, ch. 14, p. 233.
2. THE HISTORY AND THE LIFE AND SUFFERINGS OF JOHN WICKLIF, John Lewis, p. 84.
3. Purvey's Determination. Quoted in THE LOLLARD BIBLE, Margaret Deanesly, p. 441.
4. THE STUDY OF THE BIBLE IN THE MIDDLE AGES, Beryl Smalley, p. 36.
5. THE LOLLARD BIBLE, p. 132.
6. De Veritate Sacrae Scripturae, I, 109.
7. MEDIEVAL PANORAMA, G. G. Coulton, p. 683.
8. De Officio Pastorali, Trans. Ford Lewis Battles in Library of Christian Classics, vol. XIV, p. 50.

9. A GENERAL VIEW OF THE HISTORY OF THE ENGLISH BIBLE, B. F. Westcott, p. 15.

10. Quoted by Gilpin, THE LIVES OF JOHN WYCLIF AND THE MOST EMINENT OF HIS DISCIPLES, p. 38.

11. Forshall and Madden, I, xxiii.

12. Ibid., p. 84.

13. Ibid., p. 57.

14. Ibid., xxii.

15. SELECT ENGLISH WORKS, vol. III, p. 495.

16. JOHN WYCLIFFE AND THE BEGINNINGS OF ENGLISH NONCONFORMITY, K. B. McFarlane, p. 149.

17. RECORDS OF THE ENGLISH BIBLE, A. W. Pollard, p. 2.

18. Knighton, II, pp. 151-2.

19. E.g. by Dr. Gasquet in ENGLISH HISTORICAL REVIEW for July 1894.

20. WICLIF'S PLACE IN HISTORY, Montagu Burrows, p. 5.

21. CAMBRIDGE HISTORY OF ENGLISH LITERATURE, vol. II, p. 62.

22. ENGLISH HISTORICAL REVIEW, July, 1894.

23. SELECT ENGLISH WORKS, vol. I, p. 209.

24. BOOK OF FAITH, p. 119.

25. SELECT ENGLISH WORKS, vol. III, p. 184.

26. THE SIGNIFICANCE OF THE LOLLARD BIBLE, Margaret Deanesly, p. 23.

27. THE FAITH OF THE CHRISTIAN CHURCH, G. Aulén, p. 360.

28. *De Veritate Sacrae Scripturae*, I, 22.

29. Ibid., p. 34.

30. Ibid., p. 268.

31. Ibid., II, 170.

32. Ibid., III, 242.

33. Ibid., I, 155.

34. Ibid., p. 37.

35. Ibid., p. 273.

36. Ibid., p. 344.

37. Ibid., p. 218.

38. Ibid., p. 397.

39. HOLY WRIT OR HOLY CHURCH, George H. Tavard.

40. Ibid., p. 41.

41. In *Les sources de la doctrine chrétienne.*
42. *Scriptura sola;* WYCLIF AND HIS CRITICS, Michael Hurley, S.J.
43. JOURNAL OF THEOLOGICAL STUDIES, vol. XIII, part I, April, 1962, p. 194.
44. *De Veritate Sacrae Scripturae,* I, 60.
45. Ibid., II, 156.
46. SELECT ENGLISH WORKS, vol. III, p. 143.
47. Ibid., p. 144.
48. Ibid., p. 144.
49. Trans. Ford Lewis Battles, p. 48.
50. SELECT ENGLISH WORKS, vol. III, p. 464.
51. *Sermo* XXXVIII. *Sermones,* vol. II, pp. 277 and 279.
52. *Sermo* LX, p. 452.
53. SELECT ENGLISH WORKS, vol. I, p. 281.
54. *De Veritate Sacrae Scripturae,* II, 161.
55. *Fasciculi Zizaniorum,* p. 7.
56. See Beryl Smalley, THE STUDY OF THE BIBLE IN THE MIDDLE AGES, p. 246 f.
57. Ford Lewis Battles, p. 51.
58. *De Civili Dominio,* I, 423.
59. *De Veritate Sacrae Scripturae,* I, 138.
60. *De Civili Dominio,* IV, 622.
61. *De Veritate Sacrae Scripturae,* I, 196.
62. Quoted in THE ENGLISH CHURCH IN THE 14TH AND 15TH CENTURIES, W. W. Capes, p. 192.
63. R. Buddensieg. *De Veritate Sacrae Scripturae,* Intro., p. xxxviii.
64. *Werke,* xliii, 94.
65. Ibid., xii, 56–7.
66. *Vorrenden zur Heiligen Schrift München (Chr. Kaiser Verlag),* p. 107 (1934).
67. LET GOD BE GOD!, P. Watson, p. 174.
68. LUTHER AND THE LUTHERAN CHURCH, A. K. Swihart, p. 121.
69. LUTHER'S WORLD OF THOUGHT, H. Bornkamm, p. 136.
70. *Ad librum Ambrosii Catharini responsio* (1521), 7:721, 12.

71. THE BONDAGE OF THE WILL. Trans. J. I. Packer and O. R. Johnston, p. 74.

72. "Fourteen Comforts for the Weary and Heavy-Laden", REFORMATION WRITINGS OF MARTIN LUTHER, vol. II, B. Lee Woolf, p. 48.

73. *Tischreden. Weimarer Ausgabe*, p. 5, 974.

74. Articles of Religion VI, BOOK OF COMMON PRAYER.

75. CALVIN AND THE REFORMATION, James Mackinnon, p. 217.

*76. COMMENTARY on II Timothy 3(16). *Corpus Reformatorum* 52:383.

77. CALVIN: INSTITUTES OF THE CHRISTIAN RELIGION, Ed. J. T. McNeill, vol. I, p. 74.

78. THE THEOLOGY OF CALVIN, Wilhelm Niesel, p. 31. For the opposite point of view see H. Jackson Forstman, WORD AND SPIRIT, CALVIN'S DOCTRINE OF BIBLICAL AUTHORITY, p. 50 f., and pp. 64-5 for the author's considered judgment.

*79. COMMENTARY on S. John 5(39). *Corpus Reformatorum* 47:125.

80. THE THEOLOGY OF CALVIN, p. 27.

*81. COMMENTARY on S. John 16(13). *Corpus Reformatorum* 47:362.

82. THE THEOLOGY OF CALVIN, p. 30.

83. Ibid., p. 24.

84. WORD AND SPIRIT, CALVIN'S DOCTRINE OF BIBLICAL AUTHORITY, p. 85.

85. THE THEOLOGY OF CALVIN, p. 28.

86. AN EXHORTATION TO THE DILIGENT STUDYE OF SCRIPTURE MADE BY ERASMUS ROTERODAMUS. AND TRANSLATED INTO INGLISH. (1529) Deanesly, THE LOLLARD BIBLE, p. 386.

87. REFORMATION WRITINGS OF MARTIN LUTHER, vol. I, B. Lee Woolf, p. 315.

88. Ibid., vol. II, pp. 113-14.

89. COMMENTARY on Isaiah 55(11). *Corpus Reformatorum*

* Quoted by Ronald S. Wallace, CALVIN'S DOCTRINE OF THE WORD AND SACRAMENT, ch. VIII.

37:291. Quoted by R. S. Wallace, CALVIN'S DOCTRINE OF THE WORD AND SACRAMENT, p. 82.

90. COMMENTARY on Isaiah 50(10). *Corpus Reformatorum* 37:224. Wallace, p. 83.

91. CALVIN: INSTITUTES OF THE CHRISTIAN RELIGION, Ed. J. T. McNeill, vol. II, p. 1156.

92. THE HISTORY AND CHARACTER OF CALVINISM, J. T. McNeill, p. 30.

93. ZWINGLI THE REFORMER, Oskar Farner, p. 40.

CHAPTER FIVE

The Theology of Wyclif

THE LATIN WORKS of Wyclif abound in quotations and references and they are of two kinds. There are those which he inserted as a matter of form. It was the custom of medieval schoolmen to support every opinion with copious quotations from and references to the authorities of the past and in this Wyclif was no exception. Dr. Rudolph Beer who edited *De Ente Praedicamentali* found in that work and the *XIII Quaestiones* almost five hundred. On the other hand, there are quotations and references (and these occur with more frequency in the theological works than the philosophical) from writers who have exercised a considerable influence on his thought. They are not cited in order to present the reader with an imposing list of authorities, but because their doctrines have profoundly influenced the mind of Wyclif and have become the basis of his own theology. We shall notice how he treats these latter authorities.

The general impression one receives is that Wyclif has borrowed extensively, but not slavishly. His debt to Augustine, for example, is a considerable one. In *De Veritate Sacrae Scripturae* he paid this tribute to the great bishop and theologian: "Among all the doctors of sacred scripture . . . Augustine is the principal",[1] and he believed that he was now "blessed with the angels".[2] In confirmation of this golden opinion we find much Augustinianism in the theology of Wyclif, but there are qualifications and alterations at numerous points which show that he was not a servile imitator. He believed in the Fall and the doctrine of original sin, but he thought in his own way of the latter as a personal act of the individual "in his forbears" and he denied the Augustinian contention that original sin was conveyed in a physical way through the semen of the male. Again, Wyclif's theology was strongly predestinarian. He believed that the true Church was the whole company of the elect fore-ordained to salvation and that the damned were also predestined, but, as Lechler points out in his study of Wyclif's theology,[3] he did not base his predestinarianism like Augustine upon original sin and the state of fallen man, but upon the omnipotence of God and His sovereign will. The debt to Augustine was immense, but there was no hesitation in differing from the master when in his judgment there was adequate reason.

The same is true of Bradwardine, another theologian whose doctrine of predestination Wyclif admired and copied. He was *Doctor Profundus*, quoted as such by Wyclif without further identification, and his *De Causa Dei* contained a doctrine of election which Wyclif was happy to accept, though by no means uncritically. Bradwardine, making much of what Leff calls the Principle of Divine Participation,[4] argued that the volitions of God were "absolute entities" and that therefore the Divine will was the antecedent necessity of every effect and so God must be responsible for sin. The latter happened in two ways. God punished sin with sin as an act of justice and, sin being the absence of good, there was no wrong in making God sin's "negative cause". But Wyclif did not allow him this refuge. "And in this matter . . . Bradwardine is understood to say that God wills that man should sin . . . and if God necessitates men to sin, then God is the author of sin".[5] Wyclif's view was that though God could destroy sin He could not possibly create it. "For he has sufficient power to repudiate and to destroy sins, but not to bring them to birth".[6] He also rejected what he, though not Bradwardine,[7] regarded as the logical conclusion of the latter's position, that man had no real freedom or responsibility, and *De Ente* is quite outspoken in its arguments against *Doctor Profundus*. J. F. Laun makes the point[8] that this opposition to Bradwardine meant the

introduction of Pelagian tendencies into the theology of
Wyclif.

Wyclif referred often to *Lincolniensis* or "the grete clerk
Lyncolne" (Grosstête, Bishop of Lincoln in the thirteenth
century), but though he impressed Wyclif with his constant
appeals to Holy Scripture and his expositions of Aristotle,
it was in practical affairs and particularly his stand against
the abuses of the medieval Church that he gained the un-
stinting praise of his admirer. There were no theological
refinements to be made in the case of Grosstête. It was otherwise with Fitzralph, Archbishop of Armagh, from whom, as
we have seen, Wyclif derived his doctrine of Dominion. His
indeterminism was quite unacceptable to Wyclif, who
though rejecting the rigid position of Bradwardine, believed
that in some sense "God is the author of every act in the
world".[9] In *De Dominio Divino* he argued that God only
compelled in the impulse to will and not in any sense of
coercion and the recognition of this would have saved
Fitzralph from his errors. Duns Scotus was treated in the
same critical way. Wyclif had some sympathy with his
emphasis on the sovereign will of God, but when he insisted
that this meant unquestioning obedience to the Roman
Church in all matters of faith and morals, he parted company
with him.

Such sources then as he used for his theology he used with
discrimination. Although influenced by many, and considerably by a few, he passed all his material through the
fine sieve of his alert and critical mind.

There are large tracts of the theology of Wyclif which
occasion no comment either because they contain nothing
original or because if they do they are so abstract and
academic that they are doomed to lie forgotten in the copious
pages of his Latin works. So we turn to that part of his
theology which has a claim to be considered as a contribution
to Reform, and in the first place attention must be given to
his doctrine of Predestination, as rigid a one as can be found
outside of Calvin. *Joannes Augustini* was his proudest title
and, as was the case with his master, the doctrine was formed

within the context of disasters and tribulations. England in the fourteenth century was bled by wars and stricken with plagues. As the diseased bodies were buried by the thousand in the Black Death of 1349 the questions sprang only too quickly to the lips of the survivors—"Is this dreadful scourge the will of God?" "Why should one be taken and the other left?" The plague was of such magnitude that the theological climate could not fail to be affected by it and the questions it evoked. Predestination found a hearing in such a climate and that in spite of the constant attempts of the clergy and popular writers to attribute the plague to man's misuse of his God-given freewill and the punishment which that deserved.

Although Wyclif moved in this climate it must be said that his interest and concern were not so much in philosophizing about the events of his time and providing an answer to the questions which came out of the great tribulation, though he did make the point that everything which happens happens of necessity, but rather in the relation between the will of God and the salvation of the soul. His interest was to know not whether men and women were predestined to die in the Black Death but whether they were elected to eternal salvation or the opposite. The answer he gave was that some, the *praedestinati*, were elected and others, the *praesciti* (literally translated "foreknown" but really meaning "foreordained") were doomed to everlasting punishment. About this latter class two points are of interest. One is that Wyclif always fought shy of the conclusion that people were damned beyond all possible hope of recovery. "Who knows the measure of God's mercy to whom hearing of God's Word shall thus profit?"[10] This was due to charity rather than logic. The other is that it was not merely a question of God's precognition of man's own choice of evil. Though still eager to avoid the error of Bradwardine which by the Principle of Divine Participation made God responsible for sin, he insisted that the ultimate ground of salvation or damnation must lie in God Himself.

The philosophical problem of freewill and determinism

was not solved by Wyclif any more than by other theologians who have held a doctrine of Election. It can be stated baldly. Either man is really free to choose, in which case any determining God may do is done under the influence of the finite creature He has made, or else a man's destiny is determined totally and uninfluenced by God and Bradwardine was right. Either God is limited by man or else He is responsible for sin. To look at it from the human side, either man is free, in which case the sovereign will of God disappears, or else he is determined, in which case he has no responsibility for his acts. From these dilemmas Wyclif found no logical way out, but like a good theologian he was content to assert two truths which were logically incompatible in the faith that a higher synthesis waits to be revealed. He declared for the sovereign will of God and in this, as in the complementary disregard of the doctrine of the Fall, he was influenced by Duns Scotus. His refuge was that God necessitates actions which are themselves neither right nor wrong and what guilt there may be resides in the intention. There is no sin in the hand that strikes nor the sword that cuts but only "in the disposition of the subject".[11] "God looks principally to the rightness of the motive".[12] He also declared for the freedom and responsibility of man. "The wise God created man good, and with a free will".[13] "Each man shall hope to come to bliss and if he live feebly and make this hope false, he is himself the cause why his hope is such".[14] Wyclif thought it quite possible that the creature may influence the Creator's will, though this was not a matter of coercion, but rather the creature and the Creator together determining the divine volition. In no sense was it "the eternal will of God being caused by the will of a finite creature".[15] The only qualification to be made is that as Wyclif grew older the sovereign will of God loomed larger in his thought than the freewill of man.

Wyclif's replies to the objections urged against his predestinarianism are no more and no less convincing than most. People argued that if the doctrine of Election were true, preaching, which was a particular concern of Wyclif's,

98

would no longer be necessary. "Good men should be saved though no preaching be, for they may not perish as God saith and some wicked men should never come to bliss for all the preaching on earth".[16] To this he could only reply that it was predetermined that they should be saved through preaching. "So God hath ordained them to come to bliss by preaching and keeping of God's word".[17] The Pope could have used exactly the same answer to Wyclif's argument that indulgences were unnecessary because they could have no effect on the salvation of the elect or the perdition of the damned.

Wyclif contended that no man could be sure of his own election. "If the Pope asked me whether I were ordained to be saved or predestinate I would say that I hope so, but I would not swear it".[18] He made two points. One was that the only relevant test was not credal fidelity nor ecclesiastical position but Christian morality in daily life, a test which made assurance on the part of the individual concerned almost an impossibility. When the question of final perseverance was raised the impossibility was complete. The other was that people should act on the assumption that they belonged to the elect. "As each man shall hope that he shall be saved in bliss so he should suppose that he is a limb of holy church".[19] This in the circumstances was asking much. He then passed to the assertion that no man could be certain of the election of another, for how could anyone know who will persevere to the end? This he thought an advantage for it saved men from censoriousness and was a fatal objection to those two practices which he disliked on other grounds, canonization and excommunication.

The doctrine of the Church therefore which Wyclif held, was that the true Church of Christ consisted of the whole body of those elected by God to salvation, the "congregation of all the predestinate".[20] Here a distinction must be made between the true Church and the visible organized Church of Rome. It was the former which in its famous threefold division, "part triumphant in heaven, part sleeping in purgatory and part militant on earth",[21] was composed only of those who were members of the *praedestinati* and "had none of the reprobate as part of it".[22] The elect were *the* Church, and their membership could not be jeopardized even by mortal sin for they had continually *fidem gracia predestinacionis formatam*, and this was enough to keep them in membership of the true Church, even if their membership in the visible Church should lapse. One can understand why a writer like Yves M. J. Congar refers without much sympathy to "the purely spiritual ecclesiology of Wyclif".[23] The influence of his realist philosophy is felt at this point, for it was the Church as the idea of God, as a "universal", which was the true Church of Christ. It was of this invisible Church that he wrote in hard, dogmatic passages like this, which abound in his works both Latin and English: "And here we believe that each member of holy Church shall be saved with Christ as each member of the fiend is damned".[24]

On the other hand, the visible Church with its centre at Rome included both the sheep and the goats. Both *praedestinati* and *praesciti* could kneel side by side at the same Mass, neither knowing for sure which was which but one being a member of *unum corpus Christi* and the other a member of *unum corpus diaboli*. The Church visible included both the *ecclesia malignatium* and the Holy Church of God and the members of both were mixed like wheat and chaff. This Wyclif stated at the beginning of *De Ecclesia*, using the rather earthy illustration of the body (the Church) and the waste (the reprobate) which though in the body is not of it.

A distinction of this kind required clarity in writing so that there was no doubt which church was being referred to on each occasion, and Wyclif was sometimes less than clear. However, he made it plain enough that the doctrine carried some important consequences. For one thing it meant that membership in the organized and visible Church of Rome was no guarantee at all of membership in the true Church of the elect. Even the Pope himself could not count on being numbered with the saints. "For no pope that now lives knows whether he is of the Church or whether he is a limb of the fiend to be damned with Lucifer".[25] The company of "all men and women living in this world that should be saved"[26] was not identical with those who belonged to the visible, Roman Church, and this view was a point of departure from the generally accepted beliefs of the time. Another consequence was a tendency towards destroying the difference between clergy and laity; and although Wyclif did not go so far as the doctrine of the priesthood of all believers he would obviously rate a layman who belonged to the *praedestinati* as nearer the kingdom of heaven than a priest, bishop, cardinal or pope who belonged to the *praesciti*.

Finally, this doctrine of the Church brought a strong element of individualism into the theology of Wyclif. One notices in his doctrine of Dominion the immediate and direct responsibility of the tenant to his Lord. Buddensieg writes with Protestant fervour of his translation of the Bible achieving "the liberation of the individual from the hands of the priest, the Right of Private Judgment . . . and the transfer of the ultimate authority in religious matters from the Papal Church to the single believer".[27] Individualism is just as marked in this doctrine of the Church. The predestination at the root of it was something which no priest could give and no priest could take away. It was given or withheld by God to the individual. As R. L. Poole points out,[28] "individualism" in its modern sense Wyclif could not have understood and for him the individual Christian was nothing outside the Body of Christ. But as he did not identify the Body of Christ with the Church visible and as membership of the Church invisible was a little nebulous, for religion to be real and satisfying what is now called an I-Thou relationship between man and God was a necessity. What now mattered supremely was not the One, Holy, Catholic, Apostolic Church throughout all the world, but the relation of the individual soul to God.

We turn to the eucharistic theology of Wyclif and immediately we find ourselves in the deep waters of scholastic philosophy, for his first and fundamental objection to the doctrine of Transubstantiation was a philosophical one. He was a Realist and in the fourteenth century that meant that he believed that universals[29] had a real existence (the "horse" behind all horses was a real "horse") and were not merely convenient abstractions. Ideas, in the Platonic sense, had reality. "Justice, truth and goodness exist as such, apart from the just, true and good things which share them".[30] These universals or archetypes, variously called *ydee*, *raciones* or *exemplares*, were created by and are co-eternal with God and they share *being* with Him, *being* which in turn has been passed on to the singulars. Wyclif realized the danger that such philosophy would lead to pantheism and he was most concerned to maintain that universals were creatures and therefore inferior to their Creator. The relation between the universals and the singulars was compared, not altogether to the student's enlightenment, with the relations between the Persons of the Trinity and between the Godhead and Manhood of the Incarnation. The important point is that they both possessed *being* and that, by its nature and its relation to God, was eternal and indestructible. To such a realism annihilation of any creature was inconceivable as it would involve the cessation of *being* and that in its turn would mean the partial destruction of God.

The same conclusion about annihilation was also reached by Wyclif through his doctrine of the possible. Everything, to be possible, must have a real existence both in the mind of God and in either past, present or future time; indeed the real and the possible seem to be one and the same thing. The creation as it was, is and shall be is the best and only possible creation and to destroy any part of it would be to worsen the best possible universe, to annihilate part of the mind of God in which that universe is conceived and exists, and in any case is not possible. The doctrine of Transubstantiation which, in Wyclif's opinion,[31] involved the annihilation of the substance of bread and wine was anathema to his Realist philosophy.

In his later years Wyclif turned from strictly philosophical considerations and began to attack the doctrine on a wider front. He denied the claim of the priest "to make the Body of Christ", arguing that it was unscriptural, that it allowed a creature to give being to its Creator and that it subjected the Eternal to the limitations of time and the Body of Christ to the possibility of accident. He was also greatly concerned, as he told John Cunningham in a dispute over the Eucharist, about the idolatry which could so easily accompany Transubstantiation. "But as the fathers of the old law warned against worshipping images like God . . . so ought Christians to be warned that they do not worship that which the moderns call accident and the earlier Church called bread and wine, as if they were the true body and blood of Jesus Christ".[32] This charge was based as much on observation of current practice as on abstract argument. Consequently Wyclif denounced the doctrine of Transubstantiation as a "modern heresy", dating only from the time of Innocent III, which if persisted in would destroy *omnem fidem*. One wonders to what extent he appreciated that Transubstantiation was itself an attempt to refine more gross conceptions and more idolatrous worship, and also to what extent current abuses made him forget the proper Thomist position, for, as O. C. Quick says:[33] "In this [Thomist] theory it is made abundantly clear that the Body and Blood of Christ are not present in the Sacrament, either as in any way occupying space, or according to their proper and natural mode of being". But then, Wyclif thought that a substantial presence (essential to Thomism[34]) could and did encourage idolatry, in which case he could hardly do other than condemn Transubstantiation.

He did not replace the doctrine he condemned with a complete and fully coherent one of his own, though he might have done so had he lived longer. What he did was to make a number of strong assertions without satisfying himself, if indeed this was possible, that they could be reconciled and formed into one consistent whole. It is not difficult to enumerate these assertions.

Firstly he was adamant that Scripture should be the chief yardstick by which all eucharistic doctrine should be measured and he expressed his surprise that people were prepared to trust a decree of Innocent III rather than the plain sense of the Gospel. It was a principle with Wyclif that *dicta papalia* were only to be respected if they were in accord with Scripture, and in his judgment, clearly and forcefully stated in *De Eucharistia*,[35] Scripture repudiated the theory of accidents without a subject. The Church need not, therefore, be burdened with this "unusual novelty".

The next assertion was a doctrine of Remanence. If annihilation was denied then, in his view, the bread and wine remained bread and wine. That the accidents of these elements did not disappear was not in dispute, but the crucial question was what precisely sustained those accidents. The scholastic philosophers had their theory of *quantity*, which was that after the words of consecration *quantity* took the place of the normal substance (the only substance then present being, according to Transubstantiation, the Body and Blood of Christ) in upholding the accidents of bread and wine. Wyclif in *De Eucharistia*[36] mentioned other entities which were supposed to support the accidents of bread and wine in lieu of the substance which had been annihilated. One was "weight" (*Sacramentum altaris est ponderositas*), and another was "quality" (*Sacramentum altaris sit qualitas*). Then there was the theory of absolute accidents, maintained by Duns Scotus, according to which the substance of bread and wine was totally annihilated and the remaining accidents sustained in their existence by the will of God. This latter theory was always repugnant to Wyclif the Realist, but in his earlier thinking he was not far from the Thomist position and he appears to have used the expression "mathematical body" as a substitute for the old *quantity*. But when he wrote his major Latin works he had reached a firm doctrine of the remanence of the bread and wine, and indeed for this reason his doctrine was pronounced erroneous at the Oxford Council of 1381. He stated his view again and again. In *De Blasphemia* he argued that since universals were real and therefore indestructible, "it follows that the substance of material bread remains in the consecrated host".[37] In one of his tracts against the friars he put it bluntly: "But the faith of the gospel teaches us to know that this is very bread after the consecration, for Christ himself says 'This bread is my body'; but what fool cannot see then that it is bread?".[38] In the all-important words *"hoc est enim corpus meum"*, *hoc* stood for real bread, both before and after the words were uttered, and this Wyclif maintained was confirmed by Scripture, tradition, reason, and the senses. In all his later theological works, Latin and English, there is the constant refrain, "this sacrament is essentially bread and wine".

Side by side with this doctrine of Remanence was a strong belief in the Real Presence. *Confessio Magistri Johannis Wycclyff* opens with the Ambrosian words, "I have always confessed and now confirm that exactly the same body of Christ which was assumed by the Virgin, which suffered on the Cross, which for three holy days lay dead in the sepulchre, which on the third day rose again, which after forty days ascended into heaven and which sits for evermore at the right hand of God the Father, the very same body, I say, and the same substance is truly the sacramental bread, the consecrated host which the faithful see in the hands of the priest".[39] It was fundamental to his eucharistic theology that "in the consecrated host there remains the body of Christ".[40] Indeed, in order to prove the reality of the bread he was content to show that it was identical with Christ's body, the reality of which was to him in no doubt whatever. In more than one place he attacked the doctrine of his opponents because it dishonoured the body of Christ, reducing it, so he claimed, to *accidens sine subjecto*. In the *Confessio*[41] and again in *De Apostasia*[42] the question was asked whether Christ's body was in the host only in figure, as for example in the crucifix. To this Wyclif replied by making a distinction between *in signo* and *ut in signo*, using the former for the host and the latter for the crucifix, by which he meant to convey that Christ's body was *more really present* (the phrase is Shirley's) in the host than anywhere else.[43] There was in the bread both the reality of a sign and also the reality of the body of Christ.

In such a doctrine of the Real Presence the bread and wine could not be mere symbols of the body and blood, and of this

Wyclif leaves us in no doubt. He often quoted with approval the decretal of Pope Nicholas II, *Ego Berengarius*, which declared that the bread and wine were "not only a sacrament but the body and blood of our Lord Jesus Christ".[44] "Truly and really the body of Christ" he wrote in *De Simonia*[45] and "God's body in the form of bread"[46] was his English rendering. Christ was *in* the sacred elements, but this brings us to the most difficult question of all: how was he *in* them?

Any kind of corporeal presence Wyclif denied. "There is no corporal presence at the altar" he wrote in *De Blasphemia*[47] and they were idolators who believed "the bread of the sacrament to be identical with their God",[48] but the language he used to describe a non-physical presence was far from precise. In *De Eucharistia* he made it clear that the body was not present "as the body of Christ in heaven".[49] It was present *non corporaliter sed spiritualiter*. He was obviously anxious to avoid any crude materialistic doctrine when he wrote: "Yet I do not dare to say that the body of Christ is essentially, substantially, corporeally or identically that bread".[50] Such tension as there is between these statements and his doctrine of the Real Presence was inevitable as he came to grips with his dilemma—that if he insisted overmuch on the Real Presence it would be understood in a physical and therefore idolatrous way, but if he insisted overmuch on the figurative interpretation it might be taken to mean the absence of Christ in any *real* sense. Wyclif was by no means lost for words as he tried to make the best of both these worlds.

In so far as he reached a final position it was that the sacrament of the altar consisted "in natural substance and body, bread and wine, and in significance and figure, the body and blood of Christ".[51] Once the corporeal presence was denied we are left with the various adverbs he used to describe how Christ was present in the host—virtually, spiritually, effectually, figuratively, sacramentally and, as Spinka said,[52] there is no better word to describe Wyclif's view than the last. The one point which must not be overlooked is that whichever of these adverbs is used it must be understood as meaning to a Realist that Christ is present in the sacrament *really*.

Light can perhaps be shed upon the position of Wyclif by reference to the debate on Augustine's eucharistic position. Dr. Dugmore writes that the great bishop held that "a sign is only a sign in that it causes us to think of that which it signifies, thanks to a certain similitude between the sign and the thing signified".[53] But Dr. Parker will have none of it. He contends[54] that this does not do justice to the Neoplatonism of Augustine and to the *reality* of the Platonic *intelligibilia*, the "thing signified", and in an exchange of Batiffol quotations he produces the sentence, "Le corps eucharistique est un objet de foi, mais *il n'en est pas moins réel*" (my italics). If Dr. Parker's interpretation is right then in eucharistic theology also Wyclif deserved his proudest title, *Joannes Augustini*.

The question then arises as to whether or not the combination of Wyclif's doctrines of Remanence and the Real Presence can properly be called a doctrine of Consubstantiation. He would not admit to holding the view which he called *inpanacio et invinacio*, because it has no *evidenciam ex scriptura* and this view of a combination of substances is different from Consubstantiation only in name. He certainly believed that both Christ and the elements were really present—"this sacrament should together be bread and God's body"[55]— and he used a number of analogies in his attempts to elucidate his position. The bread and wine and the presence of Christ could be compared to paper, ink and the content of what was written. He quoted the illustration of John of Damascus with approval, that as the live coal was not mere wood but wood united with fire, so the bread was not mere bread but bread united with deity.[56] Again, a prelate was both a prelate and a person; but the most favoured illustration was, "as Christ is two substances, namely earthly and divine, so this sacrament is the body of sensible bread and the body of Christ".[57] Each of these illustrations was meant to demonstrate a real diversity in true unity. The language which

Wyclif used about Christ being "hidden" (*absconditur*) in the sacrament and the fact that he believed, as Buddensieg put it, that "the sacrament of the altar is Christ's body and blood under the form of bread and wine"[58] tend towards a doctrine of Consubstantiation; but the impossibility of calling Wyclif's view by that name is that this implies that the elements and the body and blood of Christ are both present *substantially*, and this he was not willing to concede. It is safest to say with Hastings Rashdall[59] that he had "a doctrine having some affinity to Consubstantiation".

Wyclif did not hold the doctrine that the nature of the host depends upon the state of the person receiving it, but his eucharistic theology moved in that direction. His position followed naturally from his assertion that Christ was present in the sacrament *spiritualiter*. Even a corporeal presence might not bring blessing *ex opere operato*, but a spiritual presence would have to be spiritually received. As Heppe said centuries later, "The Sacraments bring their blessing . . . because of the promise, which Christ fulfils directly and personally in believing reception of the Sacrament by the power of the Holy Spirit".[60] This led Wyclif to insist on the necessity of faith in the reception of the host. "So we agree that we do not see in that sacrament the body of Christ with the bodily eye, but with the eye of the mind, that is, in faith, through a glass darkly".[61] The taking of the body of Christ does not consist "in bodily receiving, masticating or touching the consecrated host but in the soul-feeding out of fruitful faith in which our spirit is nourished in the Lord".[62] The *praesciti*, who lack faith, receive *sacramentum corporis Christi*, much as in Augustine the unworthy eat the *signum* but do not partake of the *res sacramenti*. In *De Eucharistia*[63] Wyclif laid down the conditions for a truly spiritual reception of the sacrament. A person must be in a state of "habitual virtue", must possess the three theological virtues and have three kinds of grace: prevenient, co-operating and consummating. He must be willing to die gladly "for Christ and the cause of the law of Christ".[64] "So the whole disposition of a man to receive the host consists in sincere and grateful love to Christ and God".[65]

A final aspect of Wyclif's theology which can claim to contribute in a small way to Reform is his emphasis upon the humanity of our Lord. "The first belief that we should have", he wrote in *De Ecclesia et Membris Eius*,[66] "is that Christ is God and man, and how he partakes of the Godhead and how he lived here in his manhood." The latter drew more comment from Wyclif than the former, though it should be clearly understood that this in no way altered his doctrine of the Person of Christ, the Word, the orthodoxy of which was unimpeachable.

The best examples of this emphasis are to be found in his treatise written soon after 1372, *De Benedicta Incarnacione*.[67] Here his Realist philosophy came to his help, and in saying that God became Man he meant the universal "Man", the "Idea of Man", and there was nothing more real to Wyclif than that. The implication of this was that Christ was identified with men, and there is present the same kind of pantheistic danger which we noticed before and which was remarked upon in Wyclif's day by the Carmelite, John Cunningham, though Wyclif saved himself from heresy by his insistence that Christ was also God. From this position he was able to extol the reality of the human nature of our Lord, and the simple and moving way in which he did so made Bernard Manning describe *De Benedicta Incarnacione* as "his most beautiful book . . . a piece of great religious writing".[68] Christ's human nature is described as "a precious jewel"[69] and Wyclif rejoiced in the truth of Hebrews 2:16: "For verily he took not on him the nature of angels; but he took on him the seed of Abraham",[70] and of Hebrews 2:11b: "He is not ashamed to call them brethren."[71] God's great work for us was that in this real human nature Christ became one with us, and Wyclif stated unequivocally: "For I say that Christ is verily, completely and unmistakably a man, with any of his brethren whatsoever."[72] No theologian has believed more strongly in the fullness of the Incarnation and the ethical result of this belief was an advocacy of the

Christian way as an imitation of the love and humility of the God who was *really* Man.

The contribution to Reform made by this theology was a considerable one. Many students of Wyclif's life and work have pointed out that it was limited by the fact that he was still a man of the Middle Ages. By this they mean presumably that the Realist philosophy which lay behind most of his theological positions was altogether too scholastic and that the argumentative style of the medieval schools which he used to present his case was not an adequate channel for reforming zeal. Both of these points may be conceded, but neither can detract from the important truth that the issues which were the main concern of Wyclif's theology and on which he dared to differ from the current orthodoxy were all of them to assume some prominence when the Reformation came. Although theologically he did not perhaps arrive he was certainly travelling along the same road which the Reformers joined at a point nearer its destination.

This is true of the predestination which was central to his theological system. Calvin carried a stage further that belief in the Omnipotent Will of God and the determination of the soul's salvation which Wyclif proclaimed before him. Indeed Bernard Manning argues that this is precisely the point of Wyclif's inadequacy—"He did not perceive that the campaign against the medieval church would turn decisively on Augustinianism."[73] Calvin, coming later, did. His doctrines of predestination and election were more full-blooded than those of Wyclif, springing as they did from an intense realization of the exaltation and sovereignty of God which it was not given Wyclif fully to share. He has stated his position without the slightest ambiguity. "Predestination we call the eternal decree of God by which he has determined with himself what he would have to become of every man. For . . . eternal life is fore-ordained for some and eternal damnation for others. Every man, therefore, being formed for one or other of these ends, we say that he is predestined to life or to death."[74] The doctrine of the universal saving will of God has no place here and the Pelagian tendencies of Occam would have horrified the Reformer as much as they did Bradwardine.

Calvin, with his *decretum horribile* of which the damned may not question the wisdom nor the justice, went beyond the moderate position which Wyclif took with his *praesciti*.[75] He was not afraid to say with Bradwardine that Satan and the wicked were the executors of God's will, but like Wyclif he insisted that the wicked were still responsible for their own actions. "Calvin is at pains to repeat several times that the proper and genuine cause of sin is not God's hidden counsel, but the will of man",[76] and one of the chapter headings in the *Institutes* contains the words, "Moreover, the wicked bring upon themselves the just destruction to which they are destined."[77] But he made the distinction between the proximate cause of sin involving culpability (man) and the remote cause of sin, without culpability (God). He also distinguished between the deed and "the affection of the heart" (the seat of real wickedness), as Wyclif did. "But as God looks upon the heart, which is the fount of works, a work which is generally and in itself good, may be an abomination to God because of the vice latent in it."[78] Both man and God are in their different ways responsible for sin, but whereas man's motive is evil, God's is good.

Like Wyclif, Calvin was cautious about asserting who were damned and who were not, though J. K. S. Reid, interpreting Calvin's view of predestination, refers to "the fine and impregnable sense of assurance which the doctrine imparts to the believer",[79] which is further than Wyclif would go. This assurance is mediated through Christ. "Christ is therefore said to manifest the name of the Father to us because by His Spirit He seals on our hearts the knowledge of our election testified to us by the voice of His Gospel".[80] Or as Wilhelm Niesel puts it, "If we wish to be assured of our election then we must cling to the Word which the revelation of God in Jesus Christ attests to us."[81] In addition Calvin, by distinguishing between predestination and determinism (the latter being a temporal process of cause and effect, the former not) and by treating freedom not as the ability to do as one pleases but as freedom for God's service, was able to negotiate the philosophical dilemmas rather better than Wyclif.

Although Calvin is often regarded as the leading exponent of the predestination of the Reformation, the position which Luther took is of importance and *De Servo Arbitrio* leaves one in no doubt but that he believed in the operation of the sovereign will of God. "God . . . foresees, purposes and does all things according to his own immutable, eternal and infallible will."[82] "Luther," says Dr. Rupp,[83] has a horror of contingency, where chance or the unpredictable spontaneity of the human will might mock the purposes of God." As with Calvin and Wyclif, his predestination was not just a matter of God foreknowing the responses of men, but the deliberate action of a sovereign will. Salvation is all of God. In relation to his own salvation Luther wrote: "But now that God has taken my salvation out of the control of my own will and put it under the control of his, and promised to save me, not according to my working or running but according to his grace and mercy, I have the comfortable certainty that he is faithful and will not lie to me."[84] The last sentence shows that Luther had advanced from Wyclif's tentative position to a definite assurance.

Like Wyclif, Luther holds the reprobate responsible for their own sins. "When Luther speaks of necessity . . . he does not mean a constrained and forced necessity, as though man were taken by the scruff of the neck and made to do evil."[85] Man does it, says Luther, "with a spontaneous and consenting will".[86]

It would, of course, be ludicrous to attempt to summarize the predestinarian theology of Calvin and Luther in a few brief sentences and this is no attempt to do so, but enough has been said to show that a doctrine which Wyclif, following in the way of Peter Lombard and St. Bonaventure, seized upon and used was still further developed by the Reformers and so assumed a place of importance in the theology of the Reformation.

Wyclif anticipated the Reformation distinction between the visible and invisible Church. Luther asked the question "Who knows whether, throughout the whole course of world history from its beginning, the state of the Church has not always been such that some were called the people and saints of God who were not so, while others who were among them as a remnant were the people and saints of God but were not so called?",[87] and he answered the question by pointing out to Erasmus that the Church which does not err is not the historic, papal Church (the Church visible or, to be accurate, a part of it) but the secret body of God's people (the Church invisible "recognizable by faith alone"[88]).

Calvin made the same distinction. There is an invisible Church, whose membership is known to God alone, as well as a visible one. The latter is Catholic as long as it maintains the marks of a true Church, preaching and hearing of the Gospel and administration of the dominical sacraments, but it includes some whose profession of faith is hypocritical and who are not of the elect. "Again not all whom we now see to be members of the Church belong to it in reality. Much chaff is mixed with the wheat."[89]

It may be taken as self-evident that such a view of the Church involved for Reformation theology that I-Thou relationship between man and God which we noticed in Wyclif. Personal faith and individual experience which were beginning to emerge from the shadows when Wyclif wrote now came right out into the full light of day. As Dr. Rupp says,[90] "Luther makes it plain that we become persons when we stand *coram Deo.*"

It can well be argued that with the doctrine of the Church, as indeed with the doctrine of Predestination, it was not so much a case of Wyclif directly anticipating the Reformers as of both making use of Augustine. Certainly *De Ecclesia* is full of quotations from that source and the doctrine of the invisible Church referred to above is Augustinian. "Peter" and "Judas"[91] are both in the visible Church but only one belongs to the elect of God. "In this wicked world . . . there are many reprobate mingled with the good and both are gathered together by the Gospel as in a drag net . . . until it is brought ashore when the wicked must be separated from the good."[92] Luther is under the same influence. "He began" (in his doctrine of the Church) "exactly where more than a thousand years before his time the question regarding the Church of the New Testament had been stirred up again and never answered, with Augustine."[93] Another writer refers to Luther as "thirling theology to Augustine"[94] and the same could be said of Calvin. But the fact that these men are indebted to a common source does not detract from the case now being argued—that Wyclif's theological concerns in his revolt were the same as the Reformers' in theirs.

In the section on "The Lord's Supper" in *De Captivitate Babylonica Ecclesiae Praeludium* Luther introduced his opinions on the nature of the elements with the significant words, from our point of view, "Here I shall be called a Wycliffite and six hundred times a heretic."[95] He then went on to say that he found peace in his conscience in accepting the opinion "that the true flesh and the true blood of Christ were in the true bread and the true vine". This implies a doctrine of Remanence which, like Wyclif's, originated in a desire to believe the plain, literal words of Scripture, and there is an echo of Wyclif in his sentence, "When Jesus said, 'This is my body' he meant, 'This bread is my body'."[96] The division into substance and accidents in which one is annihilated and the other remains was unacceptable to them both. At the same time Luther believed in the Real Presence. For him, as Philip Watson says, "A Sacrament . . . betokens His real presence among men, and can be called an 'epiphany' of God."[97] Sometimes, as Darwell Stone points out,[98] this was interpreted in an almost carnal sense. "Thus in 1528 he maintained that it had been right to force Berengar to acknowledge that the real body of Christ is crushed by the teeth,[99] and he wrote in 1534, 'This is the sum of our opinion, that the body of Christ is really eaten in and with the bread, so that all which the bread does and suffers, the body of Christ does and suffers, so that it is divided and is eaten and is bitten with the teeth'."[100] As he said in *On the Adoration of the Sacrament of the Sacred Body of Christ,* and maintained stoutly in the controversy with Carlstadt and others, "This is my body" is not to be figuratively but literally understood. But at the same time he could write, "We . . . are not so foolish as to believe that the body of Christ is present in the bread in the gross, visible manner in which bread is in the basket or wine in the cup",[101] and his question, "Why should not Christ be able to include His Body within the substance of bread as well as within the accidents?" does not imply at all a carnal presence. These tensions are not dissimilar from those we noticed in Wyclif. Though Luther used the illustration of iron and fire mingling together just as Wyclif had used the illustration of wood and fire, the German believed it was the glorified body of the Lord in the bread, whereas Wyclif insisted that the glorified body remained in heaven. In 1539 he asked the questions, "What is there absurd in believing that the body of Christ is at the same time in heaven and in the Sacrament? Is that which seems to us incredible difficult to Almighty God?",[102] and as Heinrich Bornkamm says, "He ridiculed the Christ of Zwingli who sat in heaven like a bird in a cage."[103] Watson's point also needs to be remembered—"Luther's assertion of the ubiquity of Christ's body at the omnipresent right hand of God is fundamentally a defence of his conviction that wheresoever God is at work, He is at work in love."[104]

Although he believed in a receiving of the body and blood by worthy and unworthy alike, Luther was, like Wyclif, insistent on the necessity of faith in the communicant and he was more explicit in describing the object of such faith. He was much more concerned about the practice of treating the Mass as a sacrifice and a meritorious work than Wyclif was, but despite such differences it is clear that the two men stood in the same tradition of eucharistic theology. Both opposed those beliefs and practices which they were convinced had no foundation in Scripture and which led men into idolatry. Again we see that Wyclif's contribution was to pin-point the issues on which the later Reformers could spend their theological insight and reforming zeal.

Calvin agreed with Wyclif's view, and not Luther's, that the glorified body of Christ was in heaven. "For as we do not doubt that Christ's body is limited by the general characteristics common to all human bodies, and is contained in heaven (where it was once for all received) until Christ return in judgment (Acts 3:21), so we deem it utterly unlawful to draw it back under these corruptible elements or to imagine it to be present everywhere."[105] The communicant partakes of it spiritually, for "Calvin objects to the idea of a natural, physical assimilation of the life-giving reality of the Sacrament by the communicants"[106] and he emphasized the work of the Holy Spirit in effecting a union between Christ and the believer. Calvin used the word *sacramentaliter*, which Wyclif applied to *corpus Christi*, about the exposition of Christ's words at the Last Supper and said that the bread was called body "in a sacramental manner". For him, the nature of the Eucharist was determined, as Niesel says, "by the divine word of promise spoken by Christ when he instituted the service".[107] The role of the sacraments is "to seal for us and to make effectual within us God's promise of grace and salvation".[108]

At the same time Wyclif's assertion that the bread and wine were converted into "the whole humanity of Christ" found an echo in the man who wrote *"Il n'est pas seulement question que nous soyons participant de son Esprit: mais il nous fault aussi participer à son humanité"*,[109] and "in his humanity in so far as it was given over to death for our sakes".[110] Calvin, like Wyclif, had his doctrine of the Real Presence and like him he was at pains to express the reality of the body and blood of the Lord and yet to deny the "carnal mixture" of Christ with the communicant. "The material species do not merely suggest to us the spiritual reality in order to strengthen our assurance and faith, they also effectually convey it to us."[111] "By the symbols of bread and wine the real presence of Christ is conveyed to us."[111] Believers "enjoy the thing itself as nourishment of eternal life".[112]

The importance given by Wyclif to the faith of the recipient in the Eucharist is found in Calvin. "I say that we eat Christ's flesh in believing, because it is made ours by faith, and that this eating is the result and effect of faith."[113] This led him to assert that "the body of Christ is given indiscriminately to good and bad", but there is no receiving of the gift except by faith. "It is impossible that the unworthy should really receive Christ in the Eucharist",[114] a position which recalls Wyclif's distinction between receiving *sacramentum corporis Christi* and receiving *corpus Christi*.

Calvin, like the other Reformers, advanced on Wyclif by his concern to deny the Mass as a propitiatory sacrifice and it is of course incontrovertible that the Reformers faced theological issues like this of which Wyclif had not realized the importance. The meaning of Communion, the sacrifice represented rather than repeated, the Eucharist as the seal of the covenant of grace, these are fields he did not explore. Some of the Reformers, indeed, went on to hold positions from which he would have dissented, as for example when Zwingli said, "The body and blood of Christ are nothing else than the word of faith"[115] and described the sacred elements as "only tokens of communion and symbols of duty".[116] Yet the remarkable thing is that so much of his sacramental theology was an anticipation of theirs, and "Wycliffite" passages are to be found repeatedly, not only in the works of the major Reformers but also in the writings of those who later carried the Reformation forward in their own countries. Heinrich Heppe, for example, quotes some words from G. Bucanus written at Geneva in 1609 which might well have come from the pen of Wyclif. "The proper and true sense of Christ's words, *hoc est corpus meum*, is therefore this: 'This, i.e. the bread, is that actual body of mine; not substantially or essentially or naturally and in itself, but mystically and by sacramental promise; not by a single bare significance, but by a real though spiritual exhibition; that is, true and not imaginary'."[117] Heppe himself carries us back to Wyclif by speaking of the *manducatio externa*[118] which comes to believers and unbelievers alike and the *manducatio spiritualis* which comes to believers only.

Again, Ridley in England held many of the views associated with Wyclif. Like him he denied a corporeal presence and insisted on the truth, this *bread* is my body ("Is not the miracle great, trow you, when bread which is wont to sustain the body, becometh food to the soul"[119]) and like him he stressed the attitude of the recipient. "Evil men do eat the natural body of Christ sacramentally, and no further, as S. Augustine saith. But good men do eat the very true body, both sacramentally and spiritually, by grace."[120] It would be over-generous to Wyclif to describe him as the source of these Reformation ideas, for as long ago as the ninth century Ratramn was arguing that "as regards the substance of the creatures, they are after consecration what they were before" and that the change in the sacrament was made "not corporally but spiritually";[121] but he was the effective channel for such radical beliefs when all the others were blocked.

Wyclif's emphasis on the humanity of Christ which we noticed in *De Benedicta Incarnacione* and which Bernard Manning calls "the tenderness of his contemplation of the human Son of Man"[122] was, as Manning says, caught up by both Erasmus and Luther. Though Luther was perhaps a little uncharitable when he wrote to Lang in March 1517, "The human avails more with Erasmus than the divine", Erasmus did approach the person of our Lord as a great humanist would. Indeed, so much did he stress the humanity of Jesus that Baer remarked that his use of the word "Christ" "may be taken for the other nature, that is the human"[123] without any reference to divinity. This rather exaggerated point shows where the emphasis of Erasmus lay. As he wrote in his letter to Peter Giles in 1530: "In the Gospel do we not read that the Lord rejoiced in spirit, lifted up his voice, wept, became angry and was moved with compassion?"[124] The Christ of Erasmus was no heavenly phantom. "I should wish", Erasmus says elsewhere, "that this simple and pure Christ might be deeply impressed upon the mind of men".[125]

In Luther also much pious emphasis is given to the humanity of our Lord. When he described the Cross in terms of the battle-field on which the decisive struggle between God and the devil took place he was not so lost in theological speculation as to forget Christ in the garden with His sweat falling in great drops to the ground. And so on the Cross. "Luther speaks boldly of the extreme humiliation of Christ, and will not soften or blur the realism of the Gospel picture by attributing the cry of dereliction to a prayer of Christ on behalf of the Church".[126] When the believer becomes one cake, *ein Kuche*, with Christ, the Lord then becomes our redeemer and *our brother*. "According to his manhood", he wrote, "Christ is made my Lord . . . He can help me and all believers in our necessities and against all our adversaries and enemies!"[127]

It would be an exaggeration to claim that either Erasmus or Luther owed their approach to the humanity of our Lord directly or even indirectly to the work of Wyclif. That is not the point. This is one more instance of the fact that the themes which moved the greatest of the Reformers were already the concern of Wyclif a century and a half before.

It only remains to ask whether or not there was in Wyclif any appreciable anticipation of the central Reformation doctrine of salvation *sola fide*. Here we meet a clash of opinion between two considerable German exponents of Wyclif, Gotthard Lechler and Rudolph Buddensieg. Lechler, for all his admiration for Wyclif, argued that he fell far short of the Reformation position. He maintained that because Wyclif wrote of the *lex evangelica* and described Christ as our lawgiver he was still legalistic in his thinking and was "not fully conscious of the essential difference between Moses and Christ".[128] He analysed at some length Wyclif's conception of faith and concluded that there were two sides to it. One was a knowledge of the truths of Christianity, and learning and knowing the *credo* was essential for faith. The other was the moral activity of imitating Christ as the believer's response to the love of God, and this Lechler argued was to confuse faith and works. The Reformation doctrine of *sola fide* is obviously impossible where this confusion exists.

JOHN WYCLIF AND REFORM

Lechler stated his case quite forcefully. "Wycliffe . . . has not even a presentiment, to say nothing of an understanding, of what faith was to the mind of the Apostle Paul."[129] In this Lechler is supported by J. F. Laun who writes: "Other elements, e.g. justification by faith, were totally neglected by Wyclif. Thus he accepted not the Pauline but the deterministic Augustinianism of Bradwardine",[130] and by Melanchthon who said: "He neither understood nor believed the righteousness of faith."[131] Even his warmest admirers have to concede this, and W. H. Summers speaks for them: "He was very far from recognizing the truth of justification by faith as clearly as it was held by the later Reformers."[132] Lechler also pointed out that though the notion of *meritum de congruo* in Wyclif excluded that of *meritum de condigno*, nevertheless merit was accorded a place in the design for man's salvation. No sin could be effaced by merit, the grace of conversion could not be earned and there was no title to heaven through good works *de condigno*, but Wyclif believed that God would recognize good works well done, not as a right, but because that was the only fair and reasonable thing to do. However pleasing this may appear it clearly took the *sola* from *sola fide*.

Buddensieg criticized this appraisal of Wyclif's theology.[133] He rejected the view that Wyclif's conception of faith was a combination of intellectual acceptance and moral effort and did not interpret Wyclif's definition "to cleave to him firmly through love"[134] as having to do with works. When Wyclif spoke of faith as bringing "a clear vision of the truth", Buddensieg did not judge this to be an intellectual view of faith. He pointed instead to Wyclif's quotation of St. Augustine, "Faith is to believe what you do not see"[135] and reminded his readers that Wyclif, like St. Paul, used Abraham as his example of faith. He was "an example to the Jews and to the Gentiles . . . excelling in faith . . . not lacking in holy conversation nor disbelieving the promise".[136] This led Buddensieg to say that "Wyclif was not so far from the conception of faith held by St. Paul and the Reformation as he is generally supposed to have been"[137] and he looked for support to such passages as, "The apostles taught that it sufficed for Christian salvation, without ritual, to acquire a faith in the Lord Jesus Christ".[138] Certainly Wyclif wrote as if *credere in dominum Jesum Christum* were the heart of the Christian religion, and he said quite unequivocally "that faith is fundamental to the justification of man before God".[139] Buddensieg denied that any place was given to merit and in the book he was editing, *De Veritate Sacrae Scripturae*, that would appear to be so.

What are we to make of this clash of opinion? As is so often the case, there is truth and error on both sides. That Wyclif gave greater importance to good works in the plan of salvation than did Luther is indisputable; Trevelyan was right when he said that Wyclif would not have called the Epistle of St. James "an epistle of straw".[140] Lechler made this point fairly in his emphasis on *meritum de congruo* and his twofold analysis of Wyclif's conception of faith was an accurate and just one. It is interesting to notice that his recognition of the place of good works made Hastings Rashdall say that Wyclif was "more thoroughgoing in spirituality and ethics than the Reformers".[141] On the other hand Buddensieg is right in saying that the great and principal thoughts of Luther were "nascent in Wyclif's soul", though "not in the same clearness, depth and heart-stirring power as in the great German"[142] and this must mean that Lechler's words about "not even a presentiment" are an exaggeration. The assertion of the distinguished American scholar, S. H. Thomson, that "it would not be difficult to prove, for example, that Wyclif was *fully* [my italics] alive to the doctrine of justification by faith which meant so much to Luther"[143] is an exaggeration in the opposite direction and would not be accepted by the majority of Wyclif students. To return to the question with which this section started, we may fairly say that there was an appreciable anticipation of the central Reformation doctrine of salvation *sola fide*, but it was still an anticipation and did not possess the wholeness of the fully developed doctrine.

REFERENCES

1. *De Veritate Sacrae Scripturae*, p. 35.
2. Ibid., p. 37.
3. JOHN WYCLIFFE AND HIS ENGLISH PRECURSORS, G. V. Lechler, p. 318.
4. BRADWARDINE AND THE PELAGIANS, G. Leff, p. 50.
5. *Opus Evangelicum*, p. 445. For Bradwardine's position, see Leff, p. 57 ff.
6. *De Ente*, p. 169.
7. See BRADWARDINE AND THE PELAGIANS, pp. 91, 93, 95, 123.
8. J. F. Laun in *Zeitschrift Für Kirchengeschichte*, p. 354 (1928).
9. *De Ente*, p. 272.
10. THE ENGLISH WORKS OF WYCLIF, Ed. F. D. Matthew, vol. V, p. 111.
11. *De Ente*, p. 272.
12. *De Dominio Divino*, p. 151.
13. Ibid., p. 122.
14. SELECT ENGLISH WORKS, vol. I, p. 42.
15. *De Ente*, p. 188.
16. Matthew V, p. 111.
17. Ibid., p. 111.
18. SELECT ENGLISH WORKS, vol. III, p. 426 (Quoted Matthew, p. xxxvi).
19. *De Ecclesia et Membris Eius*, p. v.
20. *De Ecclesia*, p. 2.
21. Ibid., p. 8.
22. Ibid., p. 3.
23. LAY PEOPLE IN THE CHURCH, Y. M. J. Congar. Trans. D. Attwater, p. 39.
24. *De Ecclesia et Membris Eius*, p. v.
25. Ibid., p. vi.
26. Matthew XI, p. 198.
27. JOHN WICLIF, PATRIOT AND REFORMER, R. Buddensieg, p. 76.

28. ILLUSTRATIONS OF MEDIEVAL THOUGHT AND LEARNING, R. L. Poole, p. 266.
29. Defined by David Knowles as "the degree of reality and significance attributable to the mental perception of a similarity between groups of individual beings that can only be expressed by a term common to all". THE EVOLUTION OF MEDIEVAL THOUGHT, p. 107.
30. HISTORY OF MEDIEVAL PHILOSOPHY, Maurice de Wulf, I, p. 165.
31. This was not the opinion of Aquinas. He argued that a substance could be changed without being annihilated. See C. W. Dugmore, THE MASS AND THE ENGLISH REFORMERS, p. 48 f.
32. De Eucharistia, pp. 62–3.
33. THE CHRISTIAN SACRAMENTS, O. C. Quick, p. 250.
34. "The Body of Christ is in this Sacrament by way of substance." Quoted Darwell Stone, HISTORY OF THE DOCTRINE OF THE HOLY EUCHARIST, I, p. 331.
35. De Eucharistia, p. 71.
36. Ibid., pp. 183–5.
37. De Blasphemia, p. 247.
38. SELECT ENGLISH WORKS, vol. III, p. 404. Contra Fratres.
39. Fasciculi Zizaniorum, p. 115.
40. De Blasphemia, p. 248.
41. Fasciculi Zizaniorum, p. 118.
42. De Apostasia, pp. 222–3.
43. As F. D. Matthew pointed out in a communication to Professor Dziewicki (quoted in De Apostasia, p. xxxvi), in signo but not ut in signo meant that although the presence of Christ was figurative it was not simply a figure but had special efficacy.
44. De Apostasia, p. 68.
45. De Simonia, p. 243.
46. SELECT ENGLISH WORKS, vol. III, p. 403.
47. De Blasphemia, p. 252.
48. Ibid., p. 31.
49. De Eucharistia, p. 303.
50. Fasciculi Zizaniorum, p. 115.

51. *De Apostasia*, p. 119.
52. ADVOCATES OF REFORM, Library of Christian Classics, vol. XIV, p. 30.
53. THE MASS AND THE ENGLISH REFORMERS, C. W. Dugmore, p. 13.
54. T. M. Parker in JOURNAL OF THEOLOGICAL STUDIES, April 1961, p. 142.
55. SELECT ENGLISH WORKS, vol. III, p. 404.
56. *De Apostasia*, p. 52.
57. Ibid., p. 106.
58. In *Johann Wyclif und seine Zeit*, pp. 182–3.
59. DICTIONARY OF NATIONAL BIOGRAPHY, vol. XXI, p. 1136.
60. REFORMED DOGMATICS, H. Heppe, p. 604.
61. *De Eucharistia*, p. 13.
62. Ibid., p. 15–16.
63. Ibid., ch. VI.
64. Ibid., p. 162.
65. Ibid., p. 169.
66. *De Ecclesia et Membris Eius*, p. vii.
67. According to *De Dominio Divino*, p. 55, the original title was *De Incarnacione Verbi*.
68. CAMBRIDGE MEDIEVAL HISTORY, vol. VIII, p. 497.
69. *De Benedicta Incarnacione*, p. 54.
70. Ibid., p. 26.
71. Ibid., p. 26.
72. Ibid., p. 24.
73. THE PEOPLE'S FAITH IN THE TIME OF WYCLIF, B. L. Manning, p. 154 f.
74. Institutes III, XXI, 5. Trans. J. T. McNeill: THE HISTORY AND CHARACTER OF CALVINISM, p. 210.
75. Karl Barth criticizes Calvin severely for restricting the relevance of Jesus Christ to the predestinate. (CHURCH DOGMATICS, IV, 2. 520.) "A 'rejected' man", says Barth, "is one who isolates himself from God by resisting His election as it has taken place in Jesus Christ" (Ibid., II, 2, 449). This would not have satisfied Calvin.
76. CONCERNING THE ETERNAL PREDESTINATION OF GOD, J. Calvin. Trans. J. K. S. Reid, p. 19.

77. Book III, ch. XXIV, J. T. McNeill's edition.
78. CONCERNING THE ETERNAL PREDESTINATION OF GOD, J. Calvin. Trans. J. K. S. Reid, p. 134.
79. Ibid., p. 21.
80. Ibid., p. 127.
81. THE THEOLOGY OF CALVIN, Wilhelm Niesel, p. 171.
82. THE BONDAGE OF THE WILL. Trans. J. I. Packer and O. R. Johnston, p. 80.
83. THE RIGHTEOUSNESS OF GOD, Gordon Rupp, p. 186.
84. Packer and Johnston, p. 314.
85. THE RIGHTEOUSNESS OF GOD, p. 280.
86. Luther's Works (*Weimarer Ausgabe*) 18.634,21. Quoted in THE RIGHTEOUSNESS OF GOD, p. 280.
87. Packer and Johnston, p. 121.
88. Luther's Works (*Weimarer Ausgabe*) 4.189,17. Quoted in THE RIGHTEOUSNESS OF GOD, p. 317.
89. THE THEOLOGY OF CALVIN, p. 191.
90. THE RIGHTEOUSNESS OF GOD, p. 315.
91. TRACTATES ON THE GOSPEL ACCORDING TO ST. JOHN, Tract L.10.
92. THE WORKS OF AURELIUS AUGUSTINE, Ed. Marcus Dods, "The City of God", vol. II, p. 181.
93. LUTHER'S WORLD OF THOUGHT, H. Bornkamm. p. 143.
94. LUTHER AND THE REFORMATION, James Mackinnon, vol. I, p. 281.
95. Trans. by B. Lee Woolf, REFORMATION WRITINGS OF MARTIN LUTHER, vol. I, p. 224.
96. PAGAN SERVITUDE, p. 230.
97. LET GOD BE GOD!, P. Watson, p. 161.
98. A HISTORY OF THE DOCTRINE OF THE HOLY EUCHARIST, vol. II, Darwell Stone, p. 21.
99. *Werke*. Erlangen edition, xxx, 297.
100. INSTRUCTION TO MELANCHTHON, 17.12.1534. *Briefe* iv, 572, Ed. de Wette.
101. *Werke*. Erlangen edition, xxx, 65, 66.
102. Letter of 7th August 1539. *Briefe* v, 199, Ed. de Wette. Quoted Darwell Stone II, 23.
103. LUTHER'S WORLD OF THOUGHT, p. 112.

104. LET GOD BE GOD!, p. 163.
105. Institutes, Ed. J. T. McNeill, vol. II, p. 1373.
106. THE THEOLOGY OF CALVIN, p. 225.
107. Ibid., p. 212.
108. Ibid., p. 214.
109. *Opera selecta*, 1, 508.
110. THE THEOLOGY OF CALVIN, p. 219.
111. Ibid., p. 218.
112. Institutes, Ed. J. T. McNeill, vol. II, p. 1382.
113. Ibid., p. 1365.
114. THE THEOLOGY OF CALVIN, p. 226.
115. *Opus Articulorum on Art.* xviii.
116. ZWINGLI THE REFORMER, Oskar Farner, p. 113.
117. REFORMED DOGMATICS, p. 643.
118. Ibid., p. 652.
119. THE WORKS OF NICHOLAS RIDLEY, D. D. Parker Society, p. 223.
120. Ibid., p. 246.
121. A HISTORY OF THE DOCTRINE OF THE HOLY EUCHARIST, vol. I, p. 229.
122. CAMBRIDGE MEDIEVAL HISTORY, vol. VII, p. 497.
123. EPISTLES OF ERASMUS, vol. III, p. 180. Trans. F. M. Nichols.
124. Ibid., vol. III, p. 336.
125. ERASMUS OF ROTTERDAM, J. Huizinga, p. 109.
126. THE RIGHTEOUSNESS OF GOD, pp. 145–6.
127. REFORMATION WRITINGS OF MARTIN LUTHER, vol. I, B. Lee Woolf, p. 85.
128. JOHN WYCLIFFE AND HIS ENGLISH PRECURSORS, p. 273.
129. Ibid., p. 304.
130. *Zeitschrift Für Kirchengeschichte*, p. 354. (1928).
131. Preface to *Sententiae veterum de Coena Domini* in letter to Myconius, *c.* 1350.
132. OUR LOLLARD ANCESTORS, W. H. Summers, p. 28.
133. *De Veritate Sacrae Scripturae*, p. xxxvii.
134. Ibid., II, 179.
135. Ibid., I, 215.
136. Ibid., II, 37.

137. Ibid., p. xi.
138. Ibid., III, 132.
139. Ibid., I, 219.
140. ENGLAND IN THE AGE OF WYCLIFFE, G. M. Trevelyan, p. 141.
141. DICTIONARY OF NATIONAL BIOGRAPHY, vol. XXI, p. 1136.
142. *De Veritate Sacrae Scripturae*, p. xli.
143. In JOURNAL OF RELIGION, vol. XI, p. 88 (1931).

CHAPTER SIX

The Contribution through the Lollards

N O ESTIMATE OF Wyclif's contribution to Reform can be made without some reference to the Lollards, though an exhaustive examination of their history and theology is not called for.

Whether or not Wyclif personally commissioned these men and sent them out along the roads of England barefooted and dressed in their russet cassocks is unsettled. Some scholars assume that he did, others, like Trevelyan who describes them as "preachers of his school if not actually with his commission",[1] are in doubt and the modern critic McFarlane says, "The dispatch of missionaries on tour may well have been the work of the younger hotheads whom he [Wyclif] had left behind in the University."[2] The discussion is academic as far as the present point is concerned, for whether they were sent out from Lutterworth by Wyclif or from Oxford by "the younger hotheads" it is indisputable that many of the ideas they propagated were those of Wyclif. One can add to this the fact that whether or not he actually did the commissioning the inspiration behind such a movement of itinerant and poor priests was his. He was most anxious that the people should be taught the Gospel in their native tongue (*euangelium in vulgari*) and criticized the clergy both secular and religious for not doing it. He conceived of the poor priests as a way of remedying their neglect. The idea had scriptural precedent in Christ and His apostles, and that for Wyclif was the most powerful argument in its favour.

The names and careers of the first Lollards are well

enough known. There were the Oxford men Nicholas Hereford, who had been busy translating the Vulgate into English, and John Aston who excelled in the itinerant preaching for which the Lollards were renowned. There was John Purvey who was responsible for so much of the work of translation done at Lutterworth; William Smith the enthusiastic and self-taught layman, a victim according to Gairdner of "religious melancholy";[3] William Swinderby whose zeal for the cause in Leicestershire knew no bounds; Philip Repton or Repyngdon whose career in Lollardry, despite his famous sermon on Corpus Christi Day 1382 defending the doctrines of Wyclif, was so short, and William Thorpe the stalwart champion of Wyclif whose ultimate fate is unknown. These men working in the main from Oxford and Leicester were the pioneers of the movement.

A number of features characterized the early history of Lollardry. Perhaps the most significant was the loss of Oxford due to the vigorous activity of Archbishops Courtenay and Arundel, backed by the government, which meant that the movement became less learned and more popular, to its permanent disadvantage. This was partly Wyclif's own fault, for in his later years he was so anxious to see Christ in every "lewd" man that he placed less and less importance upon learning and never bothered his head about whether Oxford was for him or against him. In fact if Wycliffism had not been suppressed in Oxford the history of England would have been very different.

Another feature was the influence which Lollardry undoubtedly had on a number of the landed gentry and wealthy citizens of the realm. Men such as Sir Thomas Latimer of Braybrooke, and his friends Sir Lewis Clifford and Sir John Cheyne, the Earl of Salisbury and Sir John Oldcastle gave encouragement to the humbler members of society who were doing the active work of the movement, and Knighton has a picture hardly consistent with the Lollards' reputed pacifism of the knight at the preacher's side armed with sword and shield to protect him. Those who sat in Parliament did what they could there, though dislike of ecclesiastical power and wealth was probably a more powerful motive than zeal for reform.

Again, there was an evident lack of martyrs in the early years and the willingness of men such as Repyngdon, Aston (even if he did not mean what he was doing), Hereford, Richard Wyche and at the last even Purvey, to recant under pressure. This does not mean that they were less courageous than most, but that some of them though agreeing with Wyclif on matters like the Eucharist and the Mendicant Orders never held thoroughgoing Lollard convictions. They doubtless felt, as Wyclif himself did, that they were reforming the Church from within and not attacking it from outside and when their true position became apparent to them they decided that discretion was the better part of valour. Others who went further and cut the rope which tied them to the Roman Church may well have found what Shirley calls the "terrible isolation"[4] too much for them.

After the suppression of Lollardry effected by Courtenay in 1382 it was driven underground and the more vigorous bishops proved their zeal for orthodoxy by trying to purge their dioceses of the heretics, not without encouragement from the Commons. Opposition to the movement came from several quarters. It emanated from the King and nobles who since the Peasants' Revolt of 1381 had joined hands with the hierarchy, a relationship confirmed when Henry IV came to the throne in 1399 and began his persecution of the Lollards, from the Mendicant Orders who regarded themselves as the only rightful itinerant preachers in the land and whose scholars attacked Wyclif's opinions with great gusto after his death, and, of course, from the Papacy.

In spite of this Lollardry had considerable success in some areas. As we have noticed, unhappily for the future of the movement, Oxford was not one of them. Wyclif's works were burned there under Arundel's orders in 1410, and though there was a slight rekindling of interest at the time of Peter Payne it was quickly damped down by Arundel and in 1414 the University promised to arrest and punish all Lollards. There was success in Leicester, though Knighton's statement that half the population were Lollards is a hyperbole, at Northampton, where John Fox the Mayor in 1392 was a Lollard sympathizer, in Bristol and the West, where Aston, Purvey, Hereford and Swinderby were so active, in Essex and Norfolk and to a certain extent in London. There was a Lollard rising of sorts in 1414, the exact details of which are hard to come by. It was said that twenty thousand Lollards were marching on London where they were to be joined by an even larger number, mostly servants and apprentices, but a show of force by the King and his men-at-arms in St. Giles' Fields, followed by short and sharp reprisals, was enough to defeat what W. H. Summers called "a wild and ill-planned scheme of revolt".[5] When dealing with the aftermath of this affair the King appointed commissioners for the capital, Bristol and *twenty shires*.

An important landmark in the struggle was the passing of *De Heretico Comburendo* in 1401 and the subsequent burning of martyrs such as John Badby in England and John Reseby in Scotland. William Sawtry, the first, died in the flames at Smithfield a few days before the act was passed. Mention must be made of Sir John Oldcastle, the friend and soldier of the King, who for his Lollard convictions was in 1413 condemned and flung into the Tower of London. He escaped and organized an abortive assault on the capital which received support, though not enough, from widely scattered places in the Midlands and the South. McFarlane, who has recorded this escapade in considerable detail, makes the judgment that there was at this time no central organization of Lollardry but that "the various congregations were loosely affiliated".[6] They seemed more numerous amongst the artisan class than any other. Oldcastle was hanged and burnt in 1417. As Gilpin finely says of him: "He shewed the world that religion was not merely calculated for a cloister, but might be introduced into fashionable life; and that it was not below a gentleman to run the last hazard in its defence."[7] Contrariwise, Gairdner's comment on him in his protracted history is: "The vagaries of fanaticism are inscrutable."[8] With him passed the era in which encouragement and protection were received from the landed gentry.

At the Council of Constance called in 1413 to end the Papal Schism, Wyclif was declared a heretic, his books were to be burned and his bones to be exhumed and removed from consecrated ground. (The latter order, as we have seen, was not carried out until 1418.) This naturally strengthened the position of the orthodox in England and when further Lollard activity both at home and in Bohemia was brought to their notice they launched a persecution during the years 1428-31, and the number of prosecutions was considerable. According to Summers, "From 1424 to 1430 more than one hundred persons were prosecuted for heresy in the diocese of Norwich".[9] Thereafter in some places like Somerset and East Anglia there were sporadic outbursts of the rebellious Lollard spirit, but in the main, thanks to the alliance of Church and State against them, the anti-puritan spirit of the religious guilds and the end of all support from the rich and educated, the Lollards, poor and illiterate, were forced to keep silent though they seem to have revived in numbers at the end of the fifteenth century. During the long dynastic Wars of the Roses they found peace in obscurity and silence.

The doctrines and practices of these Lollards are of importance in estimating any influence Wyclif may have had, through them, on the Reformation. Undoubtedly they added considerably to even his uninhibited views. The petition presented to Parliament (which never reached them) in 1395 maintained that the customary priesthood was not the priesthood to which Christ ordained His apostles, that exorcisms and benedictions spoken over holy things were magic and not religion, that auricular confession was wrong and unnecessary (Wyclif thought that though it could be useful with a good confessor it was not essential), that the taking of life in war or in the administration of justice was contrary to the New Testament, that vows of chastity produced more evil than good and that the work of goldsmiths, of armourers and all arts outside the strict apostolic rule should be proscribed. Swinderby was found guilty of maintaining that a debtor who refused to pay should not be punished and that all priests had equal power whether they were popes or curates; Walter Brute contended that all oaths were unlawful; John Belgrave said in 1414 that the Papacy had been vacant since the first century: William Aylward confessed that "the Blessed Sacrament of the Altar is a great devil of hell and a synagogue";[10] John Badby maintained that any man of good life had as much power to make the body of Christ as any priest; John Seygno said that the eating of pork was a sin; John Skilley of Flixton was reported as believing that love between man and woman was sufficient for marriage, without any ceremony in church. J. P. Whitney sums up admirably these exaggerations and embellishments of Wyclif's views: "His denunciation of evils . . . became a hatred of the whole Church, his love of the Bible . . . a disregard of everything but the Bible, and his denial of transubstantiation . . . a contempt for the Sacrament itself."[11] Such fanaticism could not keep its hands from iconoclastic practices, and desecrations of both crucifix and host were reported. A stern puritanism which expressed itself in opposition to beauty of building, colour, and music, and a rigid sabbatarianism were less offensive concomitants.

On the other hand the genuine teachings of the master were spread by both public and private means. The 1395 Petition condemned the temporalities of the Church, urged the end of celibacy for priests (there seems to be no reasonable doubt but that this was Wyclif's view), declared that transubstantiation led men into idolatry, criticized the "Caesarean clergy" and questioned the value of pilgrimages and oblations made to images, all in true Wycliffite style. Swinderby's teachings included a condemnation of indulgences, a denunciation of Spenser's crusade, a belief that auricular confession might be useful but never necessary, and an assertion that the sacrament of the altar was "both bread and Christ's body"; Walter Brute insisted on the supremacy of Scripture, declared that the Pope was Antichrist, was every bit as nationalistic as Wyclif and maintained that the host was still bread after consecration: William

Sawtry opposed both freewill and image-worship and declared of the sacrament, "It ceaseth not to be very bread"; John Badby denied Transubstantiation; Sir John Oldcastle reiterated the position of Wyclif, "It is both Christ's body and bread" and at his trial denounced the Pope as Antichrist. The accusations brought against the Lollards in Leicester when Archbishop Courtenay visited there in 1389 included Consubstantiation, lay preaching, and opposition to indulgences. The conclusion is inescapable that side by side with regrettable excesses the substance of Wyclif's own doctrine, without its scholastic and philosophical refinements, was carried down the years by his Lollard following.

As we approach the Reformation an assessment has to be made, both of the disposition and strength of the Lollards in the country and of the extent of their contribution to the religious awakening. For some time it has been believed that Lollards were, as Sir Thomas More said in 1532, "almost entirely restricted to the dioceses of London and Lincoln".[12] That they were in these dioceses is true. As the biographer of Cuthbert Tunstal, Bishop of London, says, "It is clear . . . from Tunstal's heresy proceedings in 1527 and 1528, that a 'brotherhood' holding Lollard views had been long established in Colchester, and that its members were in close touch with various persons resident in the City of London who shared their views."[13] The latter were represented by people such as Richard Myldenhall and James Sturdy who stood as heretics with faggots "at powles Crosse"[14] and the three Lollards at the same place with "the Bookes of their lore hangyng abowte theym . . . And among their Erronyous oppynyons one was, that the Sacrament of the Awter was but Materiall bread".[14] So too Elisabeth Sampson who was accused of holding *opiniones blassemias et hereses dampnabiles*.[15] In the London diocese Fitzjames dealt with forty heretics in 1510 and thirty-seven in 1517 (four were burnt) and according to Foxe the successors of Fitzjames, Tunstal and Stokesley convicted two hundred and eighteen heretics in their courts between 1527 and 1532, twenty of these coming from

Colchester, forty from Steeple Bumpstead and forty-four from Birdbrook. As Strype remarks before giving the details which Foxe omits, "Heresy, as it was then called, that is, the Gospel, had already spread considerably in this diocese of London, and especially about Colchester, and other parts of Essex, as well as in the City."[16]

Within the diocese of Lincoln lay the other area generally recognized to be the home of Lollards. Their story has been affectionately traced by W. H. Summers who tells us of Amersham where "Lollard principles were strong . . . in 1414, in 1428, and again in 1462"[17] and describes to us the martyrdoms of William Tylsworth in Stanley's Close, north of Amersham, Robert Cosin the miller from Missenden, and Thomas Chase who was tortured and strangled at Wooburn. These appear to have been contemporaneous with the *Magna Abjuratio* of 1507 in which some eighty persons abjured and did penance. Thomas Man not long before his martyrdom in 1518 found at Amersham, according to Foxe, "a godly and a great company, which had continued in that doctrine and teaching twenty-three years".[18] In 1521 Longland, Bishop of Lincoln, began his enquiry into the heresies of the Chiltern Hills and it is in describing this that Foxe uses his famous phrase, "the secret multitude of true professors".[19] Summers from his local knowledge[20] gives good reasons for trusting the account of Foxe (whose integrity and methods have been defended by J. F. Mozley in *John Foxe and His Book*), and this means accepting that over three hundred people were accused in Buckinghamshire, though not all of them lived there. Typical of these people was James Morden who had "learnt his doctrine of Thomas Chase, and of Agnes Ashford, of Chesham, to whom he had paid seven visits before he could learn by heart a few verses of the fifth chapter of Matthew". His sister Marian testified that he had taught her the Paternoster, Ave and Creed in English, and that he had persuaded her for the last six years not to go on pilgrimages or worship images.[21] This man was ultimately burned. The villages and hamlets of the area, places like Ashley Green, Little Missenden, Great Missenden,

Hitchenden, West Wycombe, Beaconsfield, and Penn contained people of similar convictions.

Since Sir Thomas More made his pronouncement in 1532 some evidence has come to light, and there seems to be more for the searching, that the Lollards were active outside the two great dioceses of London and Lincoln. There were some in the diocese of Salisbury—the Berkshire Lollards—who were in communication with their confreres in Buckingham-shire, and Thomas Man found at Newbury "a glorious and sweet society of faithful favourers, who had continued the space of fifteen years together, till at last, by a certain lewd person, whom they trusted and made of their counsel, they were betrayed; and then many of them, to the number of six or seven score, were abjured, and three or four of them burnt".[22] In Ashford, Kent, forty-six heretics were de-nounced to Archbishop Warham in 1511, of whom five were burned; most of them came from surrounding villages, particularly those like Tenterden associated with the clothing industry. There are occasional references to Lollard activity in the Forest of Dean and in the counties of south-west England, but it is in the diocese of York that recent scholar-ship has brought Lollardry to light. A. G. Dickens cites the different types of heresy in the *mala dogmata* of 1536 and promises in his introduction that "all these aspects of the repertoire we shall soon encounter in the diocese of York".[23] One, of course, was Lollardry. Men like Robert Robynson of Hull who said "that sancte Peter was never the pape of Rome"[24] bore the distinct marks of the native heresy, as did Richard Browne who believed and taught that "the Sacra-ment of thalter did but present the bodie of Christ".[25] Richard Flynte, parish clerk of Topcliffe, heard and acted upon "a sainge in the countrie that a man might lefte up his harte and confesse himself to God Allmightie and neded not to be confessed at a prieste"[26]—another indica-tion of the prevalence of Lollard opinion—and in 1555 Christopher Kelke of York "had to reply to certain articles touching the safety of his soul *ac crimen Lollardie*".[27] Dickens argues that these and similar records "resemble the visible portions of an iceberg",[28] in which case the heresy of the Chiltern Hills was also the heresy of the broad acres of the North.

The presence, then, in these areas at least, of anti-Catholic beliefs is undeniable and even a writer such as Gairdner, who is anxious to play down the Lollard contribution, has to admit that "its leaven, indeed, was very widely diffused".[29] But once an attempt is made to assess the strength of Lollard conviction and feeling we are bedevilled in exactly the same way as we were with Wyclif himself.[30] Dr. T. M. Parker brings this into the open. Having given his opinion that "to arrive at even an approximate estimate of how widespread Lollard opinions were is next to impossible in the state of the evidence"[31] he goes on to say of Dr. Maynard Smith (who argues that the proportion of Lollards to the population was much the same as the proportion of Communists to the population today[32]) and of Dr. Gordon Rupp (who uses Foxe's phrase "the secret multitude of true professors"[33]); "One cannot help thinking that the ecclesiastical affiliations of these two authors to some extent determine their judgments." While this may be so, the probability is on the side of "the secret multitude", for though the proportion of Lollards arraigned before the authorities was small, their existence must testify to a larger number of sympathizers, and if the work which A. G. Dickens has done on the York diocese is repeated elsewhere the known numbers of both groups may well be considerably increased.

The precise extent and the exact occasions of the contacts between this native protestantism and the new importation from the Continent is a story not yet told, but there are some indications of its outline. Meetings between the "known men" of Lollardry and the new sect of Anabaptists seem likely to have happened and Summers with his local knowledge thinks that this accounts for the fact that "in some of the districts where Lollardry had been strongest, and notably in South Bucks, we find Baptists numerous in the next century".[34] But few such contacts could have been made before 1550 because Anabaptists who came from the

Netherlands before that date "were soon banished from the country or burned to death".[35]

That Lollards were open to new influences we notice from their presence at Oxford listening to Colet, "nodding or exchanging patronizing glances during his sermons",[36] and this was to be their attitude when the main stream of Reformation thought began to flow in from the Continent. They received their new allies gladly. Foxe records a number of Lollards from the Chiltern Hills accused in 1530 "for being together in John Taylor's house at Hichenden, and there hearing Nicholas Field of London, read a parcel of Scripture in English unto them, who there expounded to them many things; as that they that went on pilgrimages were accursed: that it booted not to pray to images, etc., etc.,"[37] As Summers points out,[38] the man Field had been in Germany and could tell them what was happening there. Again, Foxe, after recounting the errors of John Ryburn, accused at Roshborough (Risborough) in 1530, adds the interesting comment: "Thomas Lound, priest, who had been with Luther two years, being afterwards cast into the Fleet at London, was a great instructor of this John Ryburn".[39]

It might well be that Thomas Bilney's martyrdom in the Lollard's Pit at Norwich was not the only connection between the old nonconformity and the group of Cambridge scholars who met in the "White Horse" (nicknamed "Little Germany" because of the welcome with which Reformed ideas were there received). Certainly we have to take into consideration the meeting between Friar Robert Barnes, who when he was twenty-three was the leading member of "Little Germany", and the Lollards from Steeple Bumpstead, at which he sold them printed copies of Tyndale's New Testament; and also the fact that Thomas Bilney preached to the Lollard communities in East Anglia. The number of young men at Cambridge who were involved ("We could make a list of some fifty or sixty members of the University who might have been of their company" says Dr. Rupp[40]), their widely differing characters and backgrounds (George Joye and Bale the "sincere fanatics",[41] Fox and Heath with their "more numerous social contacts"[41]) and the variety of their subsequent careers (two became Archbishops and seven bishops, but one wrote tragedies and another was "a wild Anabaptist"[42]) make it seem unlikely that there were no contacts at all between these intellectuals and the more ignorant Lollards of town and countryside, but at this point we enter the realm of guesswork.

Mention must also be made at this point of the Christian Brethren who, much to the annoyance of Sir Thomas More, disseminated Reformation literature wherever they could find a market for it. They included Lollards for, as Dr. Rupp points out, "there are depositions in the courts in which the names 'known men' and 'Christian Brethren' are almost used interchangeably".[43] The company of Christian Brethren "who appear to have financed some of the early English Protestant literature and may have been behind Tyndale's translation of the New Testament, was of Lollard origin or at least contained Lollards".[44] So it formed a link between the Reformation proper and the "known men" of the earlier period.

However scanty may be the evidence for personal contact between those who had absorbed Reformation teaching on the Continent and those who had watched and waited with dogged determination at home, the fact that one movement was caught up into the other is widely attested by students of the period. "Dissidence", writes Dr. T. M. Parker, "received reinforcement from abroad."[45] A writer of the last century[46] chides "modern historians" for believing that "Lollardry was dead, when Lutheranism or Protestantism was born" and this in spite of their normal insistence on the evolutionary character of the history of religion. He was right. They made exactly the same mistake as the Catholic reformers of the sixteenth century who "never thought that it [Lollardry] could be galvanised into life by the infiltration of German theology".[47] "It was", says Dr. Maynard Smith in another book,[48] "an error to suppose that the sect was all but extinct." On the contrary, Lollardry existed in its own right "quite independent of the light which appeared on the

Continent".[49] But through contacts which have not yet been made the subject of a full historical study one movement coalesced with the other, producing what A. G. Dickens calls a " 'mixed' popular heresy"[50]—the result of "a diffused but inveterate Lollardry revivified by contact with Continental Protestantism".[51]

We must now ask what exactly was the contribution which Lollardry was able to bring to be added to that which came from abroad. It must be admitted that as far as the central *sola fide* position is concerned Lollard theology never progressed much further than the rudimentary efforts of Walter Brute, an early Lollard who had picked up more than a smattering of learning, and who made a sharper distinction between faith and works than Wyclif did. In this direction the movement had nothing to contribute. The amalgam of theology and practice which went under the name of Lollardry can be summarized under four headings.

First there was a deep-seated, conscientious objection to a considerable number of Catholic practices. Cranmer's own interpretation of the intention behind "The Institution of a Christian Man" (1537) was that "if men will indifferently read these late declarations, they should well perceive that purgatory, pilgrimages, praying to saints, images, holy bread, holy water, holy days, merits, works, ceremonies and such other be not restored to their late accustomed uses".[52] This element of the Reformation, though substantiated from abroad, was a native contribution from Lollardry. When Pecock made his unfortunate (for him) but reasoned attempt to counteract Lollard influence in the middle of the fifteenth century these were exactly the kind of things he cited. He informs us that the Lollards were opposed to image-worship, pilgrimages, degrees of rank amongst the clergy, the invocation of the saints and the use of ornaments in divine service. The evidence for these Lollard objections is not hard to come by, and one or two examples will suffice. In 1462 William Aylward of Henley noticed pilgrims passing his forge on their way to Canterbury and made the forthright comment, "They go offering their souls to the devil",[53] to which he later added the further crude judgments that confession was only maintained by the priests for purposes of immorality and that the Pope would lie deeper in hell than Lucifer. John Pykes, a Lollard of Colchester, who was arraigned before the Bishop of London in 1527, is typical of many.

> Also he says that he taught, rehearsed and affirmed, before all the said persons, and in their houses at sundry times, against the sacrament of Baptism, saying, that there should be no such things; for there is no baptism, but of the Holy Ghost . . . Also he says that he has in the places and presence aforesaid, spoken against the sacrament of confession, saying, that it was sufficient for a man that had offended to show his sins privately to God, without confession made to a priest . . . Also he says [and he attributes this to Bilney's sermons] that it was but folly for a man to go on pilgrimages for saints; for they are but stocks and stones . . . and also that men should pray only to God, and to no saints . . . also he says, that he has oftentimes spoken against fasting . . . also against holy days . . . but that God never made holy days, but the Sunday . . . also he confesseth that he has spoken . . . against pardons, saying, and affirming that pardons granted by the Pope, or other men of the Church, are of no effect.[54]

These objections and protests were very common in Lollard areas and the English Reformation had to reckon with them.

The second contribution of the Lollards was their distinctive attitude to the Eucharist—distinctive both by its rejection of Catholic theology and practice and by its difference from the Lutheran doctrine of the Real Presence. As one would expect amongst uneducated people, this attitude was much more a vehement protest against what was considered idolatry than it was a coherent eucharistic theology. The one thing they were clear about was that there was no corporeal presence of Christ in the sacrament of the altar, and this protestation is made time and time again in the course of their trials. *Wycklyffe's Wycket*, which had for long been part of the staple diet of the Lollards, contains the basis of their position. "Therefore all the sacraments that are left here in earth are but reminders of the body of Christ, for a sacrament is no more to say, but a sign or reminder of a thing passed or a thing to come"[55]—a statement which immediately disqualifies Wyclif from the authorship. This is a more radical position than that adopted in the early Lollard treatise, *An Apology for Lollard Doctrines,* which speaks in true Wycliffite fashion of "the visible species of elements, and invisible flesh and blood of our Lord Jesus Christ".[56] But as the Reformation approached it became clear from all that Lollards said that they took their stand on the position of *Wycklyffe's Wycket.* "The crime against Thomas Colins (of Ginge)", writes Foxe,[57] quoting from the Registers of Bishop Longland, "was, that for eight years past this Thomas Colins the father had taught this John his son, in the presence of his mother . . . that he should not worship the sacrament of the altar as God, for that it was but a token of the Lord's body." So again John Edmunds of Burford "did detect Philip Brabant . . . for saying that the sacrament of the altar was made in the remembrance of Christ's own body, but it was not the body of Christ".[58] In his abjuration in the diocese of York in 1512 Roger Gargrave admitted "further more showing and openly affirming that the date was past that God determined him to be in form of bread" and Stephen Swallow at Lambeth in 1489 recanted of the opinion "that Christ is not in the same sacrament really in his own bodily presence, and so in the sacrament is not the very body of Christ".[59]

As might be expected, there were exaggerations of these positions. Foxe quotes a fanciful explanation of the Institution. "Christ . . . took bread, and blessed, and brake, and gave to his disciples, and said 'Eat ye this' reaching forth his arm, and showing the bread in his hand; and then noting his own natural body, and touching the same, and not the bread consecrated, 'This is my body, which shall be betrayed for you'."[60] Wild things were said. Abraham Water of Colchester declared, "I can make of a piece of bread the body of Almighty God, as well as the best Priest of them all"[61] and stories were circulated about renegade priests who put a mouse into the pyx.[62] But considered as a whole the Lollard position, though a fair distance removed from orthodoxy, was stated without immoderation and was in these later years unaccompanied by iconoclastic practices.

The third emphasis of the Lollards was on the reading of the Scriptures in English. As Sir F. M. Powicke says,[63] "The use of the Scriptures as the authority which justified most of the great changes in England, and the fervent interest in Biblical study shown by Cranmer and the reforming party in the Church had made the publication of the English Bible under official sanction simply a question of time, and the limitations upon its circulation a matter of expediency. Further, the revival of Biblical study was part of what is sometimes termed the Christian renaissance as a whole." To this state of affairs the Lollards had made no small contribution. Here one sees the emphases of Wyclif himself with more clarity and with less distortion than in any other field. The Lollards recognized the necessity of Bible knowledge and if it could not be read, then it must be learnt by heart. So Agnes Wellis in the diocese of Lincoln was detected of her brother "for learning the epistle of St. James in English of Thurston Littlepage".[64] (Dr. Rupp has pointed out[65] that the epistle of James was more popular amongst the "known men" than any other book; an indication of the difference between their theology and that of the continental Reformers.) Again, "The said Thomas Holmes also detected John Butler, carpenter; Richard Butler; William King of Uxbridge: these three sat up all night in the house of Durdant of Iver Court by Staines, reading all the night in a book of Scripture."[66] English Scriptures were passed from one to another. In Chesham John Grosar received a copy of the Gospels in English from Thomas Tykill, "morrow-mass priest in milk-Street",[67] and afterwards lent it to Thomas Spencer and his wife, who in turn lent it to John Knight. Strype tells the same story as Foxe. In Colchester "John Stacy of Coleman-street, bricklayer, kept a man in his house, whose name was John, to write the Apocalypse in English"[68] and in the same town the accuser of Marion Matthew said that "he hath heard her speak of the Epistles and Gospels (and had them well by heart) in her own house".[69]

"The whole of Lollardry", writes Margaret Deanesly, "rested upon the popularization of the New Testament"[70] and the Lollards themselves knew just how true this was. The reason behind this was, as with Wyclif himself, that such doctrinal positions as they had were founded upon the letter of Holy Scripture. Most of these were negative, e.g. no Transubstantiation, no indulgences, no auricular confession, no purgatory, but they were so precisely because of their absence from the Bible. The Lollards never solved satisfactorily what Margaret Deanesly calls "the crucial problem of interpretation"[71] and Pecock was right in his criticism that to expect the ordinary, humble Christian to understand Scripture for himself was asking too much. In fact interpretation tended to become corporate and a body of Lollard "tradition" grew up, much to the displeasure of Gairdner, who wrote with little sympathy for the "new Church of humble-minded men"[72] which this Scriptural tradition produced.

It can well be imagined what a stimulant it was to a movement like this to have made available to it printed copies of the New Testament. The first copies of Tyndale's New Testament reached England in 1526 to circulate quietly and cautiously amongst those who were eager for Reform. "There were many such, especially in London and the eastern counties, successors of the old Lollards, men often in humble station, who treasured manuscript copies of the scripture, and would meet together in their houses to read and to pray."[73] The class immediately affected were "the less educated Lollards who could not read the Latin Bible",[74] but very soon men of an open mind from all classes were involved, and when attempts to suppress the version had failed "wise men were coming to the conclusion that the only thing to be done was to issue an authorised New Testament in English".[75] The story could be carried on until the issue of the Great Bible in 1539, and W. H. Summers writes of "the joy with which the Lollards would hail the newly-granted liberty, though this joy may have been damped by the discovery that the new version differed so much from their long-prized parchment scrolls".[76]

With the English Scriptures, we must, in the fourth place, link the other vernacular tracts which the Lollards read and distributed. "These were detected", writes Foxe[77] of some of the Amersham Lollards, "for carrying about certain books in English." Usually the titles are not mentioned and we have only "another great book of Andrew Fuller", "another little book of Thomas Man", to enlighten us. "Four other sheets of paper written in English, containing matter against the Romish religion"[78] is not as explicit as one would like. Books "speaking of the ten plagues of Pharaoh" and "treating of the seven sacraments" are referred to,[79] though the Gospel of Nicodemus is mentioned by name,[80] as is "The King of Beeme".[81] There are some titles mentioned in Strype—"The most excellent and glorious Lord", *Disputatio inter Fratrem et Clericum*, "The Prick of Conscience" and "Seven Wise Pastors of Rome". John Baron of Amersham admitted to the possession of a book which contained "The Life of our Lady", "The Mirror of Sinners", and "The Mirror of Matrimony" with sermons on Adam and Eve and other subjects.[82] It is not unreasonable to suppose that these tracts contained exactly the same things as came to light in the examinations of the Lollards—disapproval of various Roman doctrines and practices and especially a view of the sacrament of the altar devoid of any doctrine of the Real Presence. The *Conclusiones Lollardorum* examined by W. H. Summers[83] at Tunbridge Wells confirms this. In one or two instances there are also references to a gloss or commentary on passages of Scripture, and they presumably would be given the familiar Lollard slant. *Wycklyffe's Wycket* was still a standard work for them and in 1517 we find John Southwick accused of having a copy.[84]

With the arrival of printing, the industrious activity of "the Christian Brethren" in distributing books, the willingness of merchants to bring prohibited literature from the Continent, and the possibility of making profit out of their sale, the reading of books became a major factor in the advent of the English Reformation. Tracts like those of Frith (whose opinions on the Eucharist are not dissimilar from Wyclif's own[85]), Tyndale, and the author of *The Burial of the Mass* were weapons in the armoury of those bent on Reform and Foxe has a long list[86] of forbidden books which the bishops tried in vain to keep from the literate public. In all this it must not be forgotten that the way of Reform was adumbrated by the Lollards who for so many years had in their obscurity treasured the written word.

It does not require any profound insight to see behind this Lollard contribution to Reform the figure of John Wyclif. His denunciation of many of the practices of the Roman Church are echoed in theirs and the accusation that this was a purely negative contribution can be levelled at, and must be accepted by, both. Although the Lollards veered farther to the left in their protestations about the Eucharist than Wyclif did, in the attack on Transubstantiation and in the doctrine of Remanence which were indispensable to a position like theirs, we can see the influence of the one who first inspired the movement of the Poor Priests. In the devotion of the Lollards to the vernacular Scriptures the link with Wyclif is very strong, for they were still saying and practising at the beginning of the sixteenth century what he had been saying and practising at the end of the fourteenth, that all good doctrine must be grounded in the Bible and therefore the wider its distribution, the better. His influence in the tracts was strong at first but there is considerable uncertainty as to whether or not he did in fact write booklets like *Wicliffe's Apology* and *The Last Age of the Church*, and inevitably later productions became subject to the varying emphases and exaggerations of successive generations of Lollards, though there are common elements all the time.

The sincerity and moral fibre which we noticed in Wyclif also became a characteristic of the Lollards. It is true that only occasionally did they deliberately choose the martyr's fire, preferring to compromise so that they might live to fight again, yet none of their critics impugn their sincerity.

Morally they were sound—the kind of people to whom the down-to-earth morality of St. James would appeal. Indeed some of their exaggerations, their insistence that a priest in mortal sin could not exercise a valid ministry and their fierce antipathy towards oaths, are due to their strong sense of morality.

There is no doubt but that intentionally or otherwise Wyclif was the inspirer of this movement. Not all its defects were his, though some, like the absence of *sola fide* and the indifference towards an educated leadership, certainly were. But all that the Lollards brought to Reform which was of permanent value can be traced back, in principle if not in detail, to John Wyclif.

REFERENCES

1. ENGLAND IN THE AGE OF WYCLIFFE, G. M. Trevelyan, pp. 291–2.
2. JOHN WYCLIFFE AND THE BEGINNINGS OF ENGLISH NON-CONFORMITY, K. B. McFarlane, p. 101.
3. LOLLARDRY AND THE REFORMATION IN ENGLAND, vol. I, J. Gairdner, p. 41.
4. *Fasciculi Zizaniorum*, p. lxvii.
5. OUR LOLLARD ANCESTORS, W. H. Summers, p. 65.
6. McFarlane, p. 179.
7. THE LIVES OF JOHN WYCLIF AND THE MOST EMINENT OF HIS DISCIPLES, W. Gilpin, p. 150.
8. LOLLARDRY AND THE REFORMATION IN ENGLAND. vol. I, p. 97.
9. OUR LOLLARD ANCESTORS, p. 71.
10. Quoted by McFarlane, p. 184.
11. CAMBRIDGE HISTORY OF ENGLISH LITERATURE, vol. II, p. 57.
12. THE REFORMATION IN ENGLAND, vol. I, Philip Hughes, p. 127.
13. CUTHBERT TUNSTAL, Charles Sturge, p. 128.

14. THE REIGN OF HENRY VII FROM CONTEMPORARY SOURCES, vol. III, A. F. Pollard, p. 239.
15. Ibid., p. 243.
16. ECCLESIASTICAL MEMORIALS, vol. I, John Strype, p. 113.
17. THE LOLLARDS OF THE CHILTERN HILLS, W. H. Summers, p. 75.
18. ACTS AND MONUMENTS OF JOHN FOXE, vol. IV, p. 213.
19. Ibid., p. 218.
20. THE LOLLARDS OF THE CHILTERN HILLS, pp. 104–8.
21. Ibid., pp. 117–18.
22. Foxe, IV, p. 213.
23. LOLLARDS AND PROTESTANTS IN THE DIOCESE OF YORK 1509–1558, A. G. Dickens, p. 13.
24. Ibid., p. 24.
25. Ibid., p. 27.
26. Ibid., p. 47.
27. Ibid., p. 230.
28. Ibid., p. 242.
29. LOLLARDRY AND THE REFORMATION IN ENGLAND, vol. I, p. 100.
30. See Chapter 1.
31. THE ENGLISH REFORMATION TO 1558, T. M. Parker, p. 19.
32. PRE-REFORMATION ENGLAND, H. Maynard Smith, p. 292.
33. STUDIES IN THE MAKING OF THE ENGLISH PROTESTANT TRADITION, Gordon Rupp, p. 1.
34. OUR LOLLARD ANCESTORS, p. 107.
35. THE EARLY ENGLISH DISSENTERS, Champlin Burrage, p. 41.
36. STUDIES IN THE MAKING OF THE ENGLISH PROTESTANT TRADITION, p. 17.
37. Foxe, IV, p. 584.
38. THE LOLLARDS OF THE CHILTERN HILLS, p. 145.
39. Foxe, IV, p. 584.
40. STUDIES IN THE MAKING OF THE ENGLISH PROTESTANT TRADITION, p. 19.
41. HENRY VIII AND THE REFORMATION, H. Maynard Smith, p. 254.
42. Ibid., p. 255.

43. STUDIES IN THE MAKING OF THE ENGLISH PROTESTANT TRADITION, p. 8.
44. THE ENGLISH REFORMATION TO 1558, p. 28.
45. Ibid., p. 23.
46. HISTORY OF THE CHURCH OF ENGLAND, vol. I, R. W. Dixon, p. 38.
47. HENRY VIII AND THE REFORMATION, p. 239.
48. PRE-REFORMATION ENGLAND, p. 291.
49. THE LOLLARDS, G. Stokes, p. 66.
50. LOLLARDS AND PROTESTANTS IN THE DIOCESE OF YORK, p. 51.
51. Ibid., p. 243.
52. CRANMER "REMAINS", Parker Society, vol. II, p. 351.
53. THE LOLLARDS OF THE CHILTERN HILLS, p. 71.
54. ECCLESIASTICAL MEMORIALS, vol. I, pp. 122-3.
55. "WYCKLYFFE'S WYCKET", Ed. T. P. Pantin, B6.
56. AN APOLOGY FOR LOLLARD DOCTRINES, Ed. J. H. Todd, p. 47.
57. Foxe, IV, p. 236.
58. Ibid., p. 238.
59. THE REIGN OF HENRY VII FROM CONTEMPORARY SOURCES, vol. III, pp. 235-6.
60. Foxe, IV, p. 241.
61. ECCLESIASTICAL MEMORIALS, vol. I, p. 114.
62. Foxe, IV, p. 229.
63. THE REFORMATION IN ENGLAND, p. 72.
64. Foxe, IV, p. 222.
65. STUDIES IN THE MAKING OF THE ENGLISH PROTESTANT TRADITION, p. 5.
66. Foxe, IV, p. 226.
67. Ibid., p. 233.
68. ECCLESIASTICAL MEMORIALS, vol. I, p. 115.
69. Ibid, p. 128.
70. THE LOLLARD BIBLE, Margaret Deanesly, p. 352.
71. Ibid., p. 370.
72. LOLLARDRY AND THE REFORMATION IN ENGLAND, vol. I, p. 206.
73. WILLIAM TYNDALE, J. F. Mozley, p. 112.

74. Ibid., p. 120.
75. HENRY VIII AND THE REFORMATION, p. 303.
76. THE LOLLARDS OF THE CHILTERN HILLS, p. 167.
77. Foxe, IV, p. 224.
78. Ibid., p. 230.
79. Ibid., p. 236.
80. Ibid., p. 237.
81. Ibid., p. 238.
82. From Lincoln Register of Bishop Chedworth (folio 62, a.t.). Quoted by W. H. Summers, THE LOLLARDS OF THE CHILTERN HILLS, p. 66.
83. OUR LOLLARD ANCESTORS, p. 60.
84. Foxe, IV, p. 207.
85. See THE MASS AND THE ENGLISH REFORMERS, C. W. Dugmore, p. 97 ff.
86. Foxe, IV, pp. 667–70.

CHAPTER SEVEN

Wyclif's Proper Place

A SUMMARY AND assessment of Wyclif's contribution to Reform must now be attempted. What did he bring which was of value and what did he fail to bring? We have noticed his capacity for destructive criticism, his fierce vituperative attacks against the institutions and the practices of medieval Christendom, and we have seen that they may be partly explicable in terms of the current coin of fourteenth-century polemics or as an expression of the turbulent nature of Wyclif himself. What is inescapable is that they were directed against real and not imaginary evils and in this lay their contribution to Reform. This negative contribution is not usually underestimated, for the reader of Wyclif is generally more impressed by his criticisms than by his cures and this is the purport of Manning's remark that Wyclif was "indeed less the prophet of the future than the conscience of his own generation".[1]

The reformative value of the attacks was probably greater in the realm of church life and organization than in the strictly theological field, for, as R. L. Poole said, the hold which his "doctrinal innovations" took upon men's minds was less than that of his "ecclesiastical protestantism".[2] Luther apparently thought so too, for he remarked in *Table-talk* that Wyclif and Hus had attacked the life of the Church under the Papacy whereas he himself fought not so much against the life, as the doctrine. Although for a century after Wyclif's death no one individual of stature in England let this particular mantle fall upon him, the Lollards continued the work of criticism and when the Reformers spoke they did not speak in an unknown tongue.

On the positive side the element in Wyclif's contribution which both deserves and receives the least criticism is his insistence on virtue in the life of the Church. He was wise enough to emphasize that whatever changes in church organization and control might take place they would be ineffective unless there was throughout the Church a new devotion to the virtuous life. Reform must be internal and spiritual as well as external and ecclesiastical. In *De Officio Pastorali* he drew his picture of the reformed pastor. "He ought to be holy, so strong in every sort of virtue that he would rather desert every kind of human intercourse, all the temporal things of this world, even mortal life itself, before he would sinfully depart from the truth of Christ".[3] The pastor or curate had to be especially instructed in the three theological virtues, he had to relinquish treasure and temporal goods beyond what was strictly necessary for the fulfilment of his holy office, and he was not to extort tithes from the people, particularly through threats of excommunication. He had not to "live outside of matrimony in open adultery" but ought to "shine with sanctity in his own person". He had to "cleanse his own spring that it might not infect the Word of God". Behind such morality there had to be, as we noticed in *De Benedicta Incarnacione*, an eagerness to follow the example of Christ. "The highest Pastor could not depart from righteousness in deed or word; for this reason his life and moral example are, as it were, a vital spirit to be attended by individual Christians and especially by pastors who say that they are the vicars of Christ."[4] This insistence on virtue, particularly amongst the clergy, was a prerequisite for any reform which was to be more than wishful thinking. By advocating it persistently and forcefully, by supporting his advocacy with the example of "a perfect liver", and by handing on to the Lollards who came after him the tradition of good honest morality, Wyclif contributed to the change that was coming.

Next, it must rank as a considerable part of his contribution that whether he was criticizing or attempting to provide solutions or simply carrying forward the work of a precursor,

Wyclif had a genius for focusing attention on those subjects which were to prove the real issues of the Reformation. The list is a considerable one.

The sorry state of the English Church which so concerned him concerned the Reformers too. As he opposed its subservience to the papal power, so did they. According to Wood's *Annals* for 1530, in that year Henry VIII sent to Oxford for Wyclif's *Articles* (condemned at Constance in 1414), read them and found that they considerably strengthened his anti-papal position. He dissolved the monasteries which Wyclif had pronounced irrelevant and parasitical, and Dom David Knowles, the historian of the Religious Orders, makes the point that Wyclif foretold the fate of medieval monasticism "with an appalling precision", adding that "the programme which Wyclif had outlined was carried through to the last detail".[5] It is worth quoting the full comment of this eminent historian. "Not only at the epoch of the Dissolution, but for an undefined and very long period previously, the monks and canons of England, with a few notable exceptions, had been living on a scale of personal comfort and corporate magnificence, and with a variety of receipts and expenses of all kinds, which were neither necessary for, nor consistent with, the fashion of life indicated by their rule and early institutions."[6] This was exactly what Wyclif had said. "There is something fundamentally amiss", continues Knowles as he writes on the Dissolution,[7] "socially as well as spiritually when a community of fifty or less men or women, vowed to the monastic life, administers vast estates and draws large revenues which are not used for any spiritual purpose, just as they have not been earned by any work of mental, material or spiritual charity." The charge of spiritual parasitism was the very charge that Wyclif made.

At the same time it must be admitted that the Dissolution confirms the weaknesses in Wyclif's theory of disendowment. The undignified scramble for possessions by the gentry inevitable in Wyclif's scheme did in fact take place and his optimistic hope that by disendowment large sums of money would become available for the relief of poverty was not realized. "The general policy was conservative and tolerant of vested interests."[8] The beneficiaries included local land-owners, officials of the Court of Augmentations, people connected with the court and the government and of course the Crown, but not the poor.

With the friars it was a different story, and there is no close correspondence between the strictures of Wyclif and the condition of the friars when the Reformation came. They were still "centralized upon the papacy"[9] but now had "little property and no treasure".[10] "In the previous twenty years", says Knowles,[11] writing of 1538, "the friars had lost almost all their notable men at the extremes of the right wing or of the left." Their ranks had thinned out and only "the pro-letariat of their class"[12] was left. "Without noise or outcry, almost without a whimper, a familiar class of men dis-appeared from English life."[13] For this exit Wyclif helped to prepare, not least by the rough edge of his tongue.

Montagu Burrows' hope[14] that, when the manuscripts of all Wyclif's works were published, the charge of his having supplied the destructive and not the constructive element of the Reformation would be revealed as false has been at least partially fulfilled. Wyclif introduced one after another the positive emphases, as distinct from mere denunciation, which later engaged so much of the Reformers' attention.

As we have seen, nationalism was one such emphasis. Bernard Shaw in *Saint Joan* puts into the mouth of Cauchon the tensions of the Western world at the end of the Middle Ages.[15] "But as a priest I have gained a knowledge of the minds of the common people; and there you will find yet another most dangerous idea. I can express it only by such phrases as France for the French, England for the English, Italy for the Italians, Spain for the Spanish and so forth. . . . Call this side of her heresy Nationalism if you will. I can find you no better name for it. I can only tell you that it is essentially anti-Catholic and anti-Christian; for the Catholic Church knows only one realm, and that is the realm of Christ's kingdom. Divide that kingdom into nations and you dethrone Christ." Wyclif would have agreed with the

Chaplain's reply; "Certainly England for the English goes without saying: it is the simple law of nature", and in so agreeing and in allowing this conviction to permeate his thinking in the politico-ecclesiastical field he proved himself to be a man born before his time.

One expression of Wyclif's nationalism was his opposition to the Sanctuary Right and it is significant that, as A. G. Dickens says,[16] "Amongst the more unquestionably beneficent works of Henry VIII and Thomas Cromwell was the virtual destruction of Sanctuary by the Acts of 1534, 1536 and 1540."

The closely allied emphasis on the place of the King is further evidence of the connection between Wyclif and the Reformation. However easy it may be to pick holes in Wyclif's conception of the kingly office—and his system really demanded not a man but an archangel to sit on the throne—we cannot explain the correspondence between his theory and what actually happened in England as a matter of luck. The fact that the English Reformation was so Erastian in character and so much the work of the Crown can hardly be attributed to Henry VIII being an assiduous reader of Wyclif's Latin works. The truth is that Wyclif for all his flights of fancy had real historical insight. It is illuminating for the student of Wyclif to read in Tyndale's *Obedience of a Christian Man* that "The King is in the room of God",[17] and to notice both the terms of the Act of Supremacy which gave to the Crown such jurisdictions "as by any spiritual power or authority have heretofore been or may lawfully be exercised or used for the visitations of the ecclesiastical state and persons, and for reformation, order and correction of the same, and of all manner of errors, heresies, schisms, abuses, offences, contempts and enormities"[18] and the claim for Christian Kings and Princes in the King's Book: "to foresee that within their dominions such ministers be ordained and appointed in their churches as can and will truly and purely set out the true doctrine of Christ".[19] Again one cannot read the words of Cranmer, "All Christian princes have committed unto them immediately of God the whole care of all their subjects, as well concerning the administration of God's word for the cure of souls, as concerning the ministration of things political and civil governance"[20] without one's mind returning to *De Officio Regis*. For better or for worse, what Wyclif wanted, and more, had arrived.

Wyclif's schemes for disendowment of the Church and reform of the clergy would inevitably have given to the laity an importance which they had not received during the Middle Ages, and again this thinking showed the same trend as events. In 1371 Parliament petitioned that able laymen should be appointed to the chief offices of state in place of clergy like William Wykeham and gradually over the next two centuries the voice of the layman began to be heard in ecclesiastical and even theological affairs.

There is no need to repeat here what was said in previous chapters concerning both the authority of Scripture and the consequent necessity of its translation into the vernacular. Referring to the supreme authority of Scripture Matthew Spinka, a modern interpreter of Wyclif, speaks of "this doctrine which *more than anything else* links him with the Reformation"[21] and this is no exaggeration. Wyclif focused attention on the crucial issue, and as we have seen, his Lollard successors in their quiet and dogged way carried his emphasis on Scripture right down to the days of the Reformation. One hundred and fifty years before the time, Wyclif seized on the one authority adequate for Reform, gave it the central place in his work and did his best to bring knowledge of it to the people, both by translation and insistence on the preaching of the Word.

In the realm of theology we noticed that Wyclif stressed almost all of the doctrines which came into prominence at the Reformation, *sola fide* being the chief exception. It is significant that of the nineteen propositions of Robert Barnes in the vernacular version which Bugenhagen published in German in 1531,[22] ten are found frequently in the works of Wyclif. Again the fierce reaction to his work, the proscription of his writings, the defamation of his name by the Roman Church and to a lesser extent the eclipse which all Realists suffered when Realism went out of fashion, made impossible those direct links which would have made the Reformers' dependence upon him beyond dispute. No copies of his works lay ready to the hands of Luther, Calvin or Zwingli (*Trialogus* was the first to be printed, in Basel in 1525) and consequently they did not read him; but of the indirect influence of his doctrines, particularly through Hus and Bohemia, there can be little doubt. The facts are well enough known. Links between England and Bohemia forged by the Universities of Oxford and Prague were considerably strengthened by the marriage of Richard II with Anne, sister of Wenzel of Bohemia, in 1382. The philosophy and theology of Wyclif in both oral and written form were part of the intellectual traffic between the two countries carried on by men like Jerome of Prague. John Hus particularly was strongly influenced by Wyclif and a comparison of the two men's *De Ecclesia* shows that Hus incorporated considerable sections of Wyclif's work almost verbatim into his own. Luther in his turn was familiar with the works of Hus and in both 1536 and 1537 he wrote prefaces to editions of his letters. He confessed to reading his sermons and remarked "How firmly Hus clings in his writings and words to the doctrines of Christ."[23] It is difficult to say how much of this praise is due to Wyclif, because Hus accepted some Wycliffite ideas and rejected others (e. g. he accepted the authority of Scripture and the doctrine of the Church as "the assembly of the elect" but rejected the notion that after consecration the bread remained material bread), but did not in his works distinguish between what was original and what he had taken from Wyclif. Peter Payne was also active in this field. In a little book significantly called *A Forgotten Great Englishman* James Baker writes, "Peter Payne was one of the greatest of the leaders of the Wycliffites (known to us English as Hussites) of Bohemia through all the fierce years from 1417 until 1455."[24] In far-off Bohemia he "spoke words of truth against Rome's corruption",[25] and he must be reckoned as a link in the chain between Wyclif and the Reformation.

Although channels between Wyclif and the Reformers were

partially blocked or closed altogether, the fact remains that
in the theological field as in the practical Wyclif's contribution was to be concerned about the precise issues which were
to become the subjects of the Reformers' zeal in the sixteenth
century. He was on the scent and going strong even if he
was not to be in at the kill.

At the same time that we recognize what Wyclif brought
to the cause of Reform we must also recognize what he
failed to bring. It is apparent that he brought no striking
gift of originality. In every important subject with which he
deals he had one or two precursors who said, if not the same
thing, something very similar. Marsiglio and to a lesser
extent Dante and Grosstête had attacked the more obvious
faults of the medieval Church, deploring its secularization
and criticizing its papal rule. Nationalism was becoming the
prevalent mood of the time, as the Statutes of Provisors and
Praemunire indicate, though much of Wyclif's thinking about
the office of the King seems to have originated in his own
mind. The theory of Dominion came from Fitzralph and the
Spiritual Franciscans had preached the doctrine of evangelical poverty. The authority of Holy Scripture was a
concern of both Grosstête and Occam, and the former had
like Wyclif a desire for more and better preaching. In theology
much of Wyclif's orthodoxy came straight from the scholasticism in which he was steeped, and for his central doctrine
of predestination he was indebted to Augustine and
Bradwardine. His doctrine of the Eucharist is so much
subject to development and so difficult to formulate precisely
that to sort out what is original and what is not would be
impossible. It was this state of affairs which made Dean
Milman complain that Wyclif had no positive doctrine of his
own to put forward.

It is difficult to see what any accusation of lack of originality can accomplish. Religion, particularly on its theological
side, is not given to extolling originality as a virtue, and
though complaint can be made and is made that Wyclif
turned to the wrong sources for his theological emphases,
if he had made them all up himself the complaints would

have been louder. He was quite original enough for his opponents. In any case the origin of the ideas, whether in Wyclif's mind or in the minds of his predecessors, did not affect the place they had in bringing the Reformation nearer.

That lack of insight into what was possible and wise and what was not which we noticed in his excursion into politics, his disregard of the consequences of events like the loss of Oxford and his theory of disendowment and return to New Testament poverty, must inevitably affect the assessment we make of his contribution to Reform. And it was not confined to those matters. McFarlane is right when he argues[26] that no kind of Reformation was possible in England without the backing of the court and the governing classes. Although Wyclif gave them a prominent place in his theoretical schemes for the reform of the Church, in practice he turned them against himself both by his sympathy with the peasants in their struggle and his strong words against the cherished doctrine of Transubstantiation. He made no systematic attempt to capitalize their natural antipathy to the rich and powerful hierarchy of the Church except by inserting them into his theories as confiscators of ecclesiastical property. In these ways he lost the services of potential, and in the circumstances indispensable, allies. However, whilst all this is factual it is difficult to see what else he could have done as an honest man. If, as undoubtedly was the case, he did have sympathy with the peasants' cause and did reject Transubstantiation as a matter of conscience, to have set these things aside for the sake of convenient alliances would have been the action of an unprincipled opportunist and whatever else he may have been Wyclif was not that. Or again his attitude to the Bible and the translation made at his instigation was of inestimable value to Reform, but one can imagine that a man with a more practical mind bent on the reformation of the whole Church would have made, even in those pre-Caxtonian days, more elaborate and organized arrangements for its distribution and reading than were possible through the efforts of the Poor Priests.

It can therefore be argued that if Wyclif had been less of
a recluse and more of an organizer the Reformation in
England might have come more quickly than it did, and
certainly his lack of worldly wisdom meant that such
influence as he was able to exert in practical affairs tended
to be localized. But surely what a Reformation requires in
the first instance is not organizing ability and careful cal-
culation, essential though they may be at later stages, but
a break-through which only strong words and passionate
sincerity can achieve. In which case when we are assessing
the contribution of John Wyclif to Reform much of this
particular criticism can be discounted.

His contribution might well have been greater if he had
been less of a scholar and more of a prophet. Wyclif had been
reared on the syllogisms and hair-splitting debates of the
medieval schoolmen, and any body of men more devoid of
prophetic fire it is hard to imagine. Since the days of Aquinas
the context in which theologians had to work had been the
philosophy of Aristotle combined with the dogma of the
Church, both under the conservative authority of Rome.
This was hardly calculated to produce bold and revolutionary
thought and Wyclif never quite escaped from the tentacles of
this theological octopus. Whenever he appealed to authorities
to substantiate some point he usually added to Scripture the
doctors whose authority was acknowledged in the schools.
The advantage of this was that he was understood and respected at once by the learned of his day, but it carried the
corresponding disadvantage of his not being able to produce
the new concepts which a Reformation demanded and clothe
them in the dress which a new age required. That he was a
brilliant exponent of the scholastic technique there is not
much doubt. One has only to read his attacks on the
philosophy of Transubstantiation to realize how smoothly he
manipulated the concepts of the schools. His biographers,
with only the odd exception, never weary of praising his
ability in this direction. Even Knighton, his contemporary
opponent, wrote of "John Wyclif . . . a most eminent doctor
of theology . . . he was reputed to be second to none in

philosophy and incomparable in the exercises of the schools, a man of profound wit, and very strong and powerful in disputations".[27] The student who is looking for the marks of the Reformer in Wyclif reads these tributes with no enthusiasm, for the extent to which he was immersed in scholasticism was the extent to which he was unable to give his reforming ideas popular and effectual expression.

We have to face the fact that Wyclif was not able to put his gospel in a way which would capture and fire the hearts of men. His stormings against the corruption of the Church failed to catch the ear of the people and evoke their wrath because they were either written in Latin and therefore could not be read by most (the cosmopolitanism of the University at Oxford is not a complete answer to this), or were, in the last years, preached at Lutterworth to a rustic congregation who were hardly likely to rise in revolt against the established order. Admittedly the English tracts (the authorship of some of them still undetermined) and the activities of the Lollards do something to modify this judgment, but not enough. If Wyclif had taken to horse himself like John Wesley and been able to foment popular indignation in the market-place against the corruptions and extortions of the Church the story might have been different. Then it might well have been true to say that every other man you met was a Lollard.

In those parts of his work which are more than mere denunciations we can see the same failure. He can spin a fine theory and set the scholars and bishops by the ears, but he has no prophetic word for the masses. His doctrine of the Eucharist is a case in point. Here was inflammable material indeed, but somehow it never caught fire. The plain rejection of Transubstantiation and the substitution of a simple and easily assimilated doctrine was made impossible by the endless theorizing over realism and nominalism, substance and accidents, *in signo* and *ut in signo* and numerous other theological wrangles which meant nothing whatever to the common people. The same can be said about the possibility of that individual access to God which might have eased the Roman yoke. Wyclif's individualism was linked to his complicated and (to the common people) quite incomprehensible doctrine of Dominion, and this could not take a man straight into the presence of God as the Reformation doctrine of *sola fide* was later able to do. To this must be added the fact that Wyclif's predestinarianism explicitly excluded any doctrine of Assurance, for this too was part of his undoing. To go to the people and expect a response one must be able, as the Methodists were in the eighteenth century, to assure them of salvation. Wyclif could offer them only a possibility and the cool advice that they ought to act as if they were predestinate. All this meant that he had no gospel ready for the people and there could be no Reformation without it.

While the justice of this criticism must be conceded there is one mistake which we must not in all fairness make, and that is to judge Wyclif as if Luther and Calvin had already lived. It is our knowledge and appreciation of the *sola fide* doctrine of the Reformation which makes us see Wyclif's combination of intellectual belief and moral effort as inadequate and his doctrine of Dominion as no match for that personal, saving faith by which a man is justified. Again it is the magnificent emphasis on the sovereignty of God which accompanies Calvin's doctrine of Predestination which enables us to see that Wyclif's concern with the relation of the predestination process to the Church visible and the wickedness of the Roman hierarchy set the doctrine in the wrong context. In the light of Calvin's organization at Geneva Wyclif's arrangements for sending out the Poor Priests were very rudimentary; and once we have seen Luther nailing his theses to the door and making his case against John Eck in Leipzig Castle, Wyclif saying Mass before his Lutterworth congregation is a small figure by comparison. But this is exactly the comparison which we must not make, and to look at Wyclif through post-Reformation eyes is the one temptation which must be resisted.

He must be set firmly against his own background. It is in the context of the medieval schools and their commanding influence over theologians, the unstirred consciences of the English laity, both serf and lord, the nationalism which was as yet in its earliest stages, the closed Bible and a Church that had ruled the religious life of the land for century after century with monolithic domination, that we must see Wyclif. His achievements may have lacked those practical steps like an open breach with Rome and an adequate organization to propagate an alternative, and those developed doctrines like *sola fide* which could both replace the more discredited parts of Roman theology and be understood of the people, but what they did do was to disturb with a severe jolt the *status quo* of the fourteenth century, to raise the loud voice of protest and to make possible a movement forward in those directions which the history of the Reformation has proved to be the right ones. When a man is successful in doing this, in the teeth of history, it is asking much to expect him to popularize his gospel and organize its propagation. Enough that almost single-handed he should have established a bridgehead for the forces still to come.

This brings us back to where we began. Wyclif's achievements and his character are inextricably joined. His intellectualism prevented what attempts he did make to put his case before the people from being adequate and his unpracticality prevented him from organizing either a strong and effective Lollard party at Oxford or a popular movement up and down the country. The criticism of Hearnshaw[28] that he was not a religious man at all is unjust. Wyclif had an appreciation of our Lord's humanity which was born not only of academic theology, but of genuine religious experience. It would also seem a charitable judgment and a sound one that the writer of *De Eucharistia* and other numerous passages on the Eucharist was not merely an arid philosopher and bitter controversialist, but a man to whom sacramental worship was a reality. At the same time Dr. Hearnshaw has put his finger on Wyclif's weakness. He was not religious *enough*, and even if it is harsh to class him with David Hume rather than John Wesley it is true that he lacked the profound religious experience which gave the eighteenth-century evangelist his prophetic fire and his direct influence over the masses. On the other hand some of his personal qualities and characteristics were exactly what were required by the work to which history had called him. His tempestuous nature and his capacity to write in anger, though not the best means of making friends, were an advantage to one whose first function was to protest. His sincerity and singlemindedness, his fearless defiance of established authority and his readiness to stand Wyclif *contra mundum* were admirable qualities in a man who set himself up against the greatest organization on earth when he believed that organization to be wrong. His devotion to the virtuous life was indispensable in one who had to cry out against corruption within the Body of Christ.

But even if Wyclif had possessed all the qualities of the complete Reformer the Reformation could not have arrived in England in the fourteenth century. The impact he made and the success and failure of the movement, if we may call it that, which sprang from his work was determined by historical trends over which he had no control. A modern historian has said that "though men help to make their history by the decisions they take, there is a sense in which they are the victims of events—caught up in a time process which they only partly understand",[29] and this is true of Wyclif. The responsible and educated classes were not ready to support Reform and it is extremely doubtful whether a Wyclif with the blemishes removed could have changed them within the space of one short lifetime. The Church, after long centuries of power, was in no shape to reform herself and the Erastian alternative of reform by the State was not ready to hand, for the separate nations were still too young. The thought-forms of this pre-Renaissance period both in theology and ecclesiastical politics were still those of the Middle Ages and new wine cannot be contained in old bottles. In other words John Wyclif was, as we all are, a prisoner of history.

REFERENCES

1. CAMBRIDGE MEDIEVAL HISTORY, vol. VII, p. 506.
2. WYCLIFFE AND MOVEMENTS FOR REFORM, R. L. Poole, p. 3.
3. Trans. Ford Lewis Battles in Library of Christian Classics, vol. XIV, ADVOCATES OF REFORM, p. 32.
4. Ibid., p. 48.
5. THE RELIGIOUS ORDERS IN ENGLAND, vol. II: "The End of the Middle Ages", David Knowles, p. 106.
6. THE RELIGIOUS ORDERS IN ENGLAND, vol. III: "The Tudor Age", David Knowles, p. 256.
7. Ibid., p. 259.
8. Ibid., p. 394.
9. Ibid., p. 360.
10. Ibid., p. 360.
11. Ibid., p. 365.
12. Ibid., p. 365.
13. Ibid., p. 365.
14. WICLIF'S PLACE IN HISTORY, Montagu Burrows, Lecture I.
15. SAINT JOAN, Bernard Shaw, scene IV. Quoted by permission of the Public Trustee and the Society of Authors.
16. LOLLARDS AND PROTESTANTS IN THE DIOCESE OF YORK, A. G. Dickens, p. 87.
17. Quoted by Gordon Rupp, STUDIES IN THE MAKING OF THE ENGLISH PROTESTANT TRADITION, p. 77.
18. Quoted in THE REFORMATION IN ENGLAND, F. M. Powicke, p. 117.
19. STUDIES IN THE MAKING OF THE ENGLISH PROTESTANT TRADITION, p. 151.
20. Quoted in THE REFORMATION IN ENGLAND, p. 101.
21. My italics. Spinka, ADVOCATES OF REFORM, p. 26.
22. See STUDIES IN THE MAKING OF THE ENGLISH PROTESTANT TRADITION, p. 39.
23. M. Luther. *Monumenta*, Preface, vol. I, 1537.

24. A FORGOTTEN GREAT ENGLISHMAN, James Baker, pp. 36-7.

25. Ibid., p. 105.

26. JOHN WYCLIFFE AND THE BEGINNINGS OF ENGLISH NONCONFORMITY, K. B. McFarlane, p. 99.

27. From TESTIMONIALS CONCERNING DR. JOHN WYCLIF in THE HISTORY OF THE LIFE AND SUFFERINGS OF THE REVEREND AND LEARNED JOHN WYCLIF D.D., John Lewis, M.A., p. xxiii.

28. THE SOCIAL AND POLITICAL IDEAS OF SOME GREAT MEDIEVAL THINKERS, F. J. C. Hearnshaw, p. 221.

29. INTERNATIONAL CONFLICT IN THE TWENTIETH CENTURY, Herbert Butterfield, p. 47.

Index